The Sydney Opera House

The Sydney Opera House

Carol Floyd & Julia Collingwood

NH
NEW
HOLLAND

First published in Australia in 2000 by
New Holland Publishers (Australia) Pty Ltd
Sydney • Auckland • London • Cape Town
14 Aquatic Drive Frenchs Forest NSW 2086 Australia
218 Lake Road Northcote Auckland New Zealand
24 Nutford Place London W1H 6DQ United Kingdom
80 McKenzie Street Cape Town 8001 South Africa

Created, designed and produced by
Collingwood & Floyd,
17 Waddell Crescent
Hornsby Heights
NSW 2077

National Library of Australia Cataloguing-in-Publication Data:

Floyd, Carol.
The Sydney Opera House.

Bibliography.
Includes index.
ISBN 1 86436 666 4.

1. Sydney Opera House — Pictorial works. 2. Sydney Opera House — Design and
construction. 3. Sydney Opera House. I. Collingwood, Julia. II. Title.

725.822099441

Designed by Julia Collingwood
Printed by Kyodo Printing Co. Singapore
Cover photo: David Moore
Frontispiece painting: *Sydney Night* by Ken Done 1984. Oil, crayon and ink on
paper 70 x 80 cm.
Title page photo: Tom Keating
Photo pages 6 and 7: Mark Lang, courtesy of Wildlight
Every effort has been made to obtain permission from all photograph copyright
holders. Please direct any inquiries to Collingwood & Floyd.

Contents

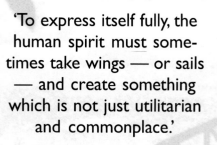

'To express itself fully, the human spirit must sometimes take wings — or sails — and create something which is not just utilitarian and commonplace.'

Queen Elizabeth II, at the opening ceremony.

'A Beautiful White Shimmering Thing ...'

The Sydney Opera House is one of the most recognisable buildings in the world, taking its place next to such icons of architecture as the Eiffel Tower and the Empire State Building. Its graceful, sail-like roofs, gleaming in the southern sun, and its superb position on Bennelong Point, jutting into one of the world's greatest natural harbours, make it the pre-eminent symbol of Sydney and of Australia as a nation. With the backdrop of a shining sea and the massive solidity of the Harbour Bridge posing a contrasting statement to its elegant, fluid lines, it is an eloquent tribute to the genius of its designing architect, Jørn Utzon. It has become known as the eighth wonder of the world; a truly unique building that broke new ground in both architecture and engineering.

One of its most remarkable features is that it casts a spell on the viewer from almost any vantage point: the

The white and cream tiles chosen by Utzon reflect the changing lights of Sydney Harbour: the tiles have been described as 'some of the most alive surfaces in architecture'. (Photos: top left and left courtesy of Ove Arup and Partners. Above: Photo Carol Floyd)
Opposite: The sculptural qualities of the Opera House are especially evident in this evening silhouette. (Photo David Moore)

beautiful shapes are as exhilarating from a distance as they are to the viewer gazing up directly beneath a shell. In its prominent position, it stands alone on its own small peninsula, separated from the mass of buildings behind it.

The design of the roofs posed a unique challenge: they would be viewed from the Harbour Bridge, the Cahill Expressway, and from city buildings — a flat roof crowded with air conditioning facilities and pipes would never do. Utzon was keenly aware of how the building would be on display to the city, explaining that 'the forms have to be sort of like a sculpture that can be seen from all sides'.

Dynamic as a living thing, its appearance is always changing: against a grey and turbulent sky its shells create a delicate interplay of pearly grey and darker shadow; while against the bright blue of a clear summer sky it is a resplendent white jewel. In a certain light it looks massive and imposing, while in other conditions it is an ethereal presence — a building that looks set to float away into the harbour. Utzon carefully researched the site and its surroundings before he even saw it, and thought of the performance centre as a show in its own right. 'Reflecting the mood

of the sky by day, mirroring its glimmering lights on the water by night, the Sydney Opera House will perform its own drama on the harbour.' Those who live or work near the building, day after day, often comment on the way that the endless moods of this vibrant structure seem to respond in a living way to the moods of nature. As Richard Weston, Professor of Architecture at Cardiff University wrote, the tile surfaces are 'some of the most alive surfaces in architecture, by turn flaring with diamonds of light; sheer dazzling white in full sun, pearlescent ... in shadow; or glowing cream, pink or ochre as they return the ambient light'.

The turbulent story of the Opera House's construction and the immense design challenges that it posed give it an important place in the folklore and history of Australia as well as on the world architectural stage. The tale of its creation is a fascinating one on several counts: it highlights the political and cultural divisions in the Australian nation as it began to be conscious of its own cultural identity; it exemplifies the eternal conflict between perfection and practicality; and it illustrates the power of human ingenuity in pursuit of an ideal.

As the centrepiece of the harbour, the Sydney Opera House is a persuasive counterpoint to the idea of Australia as a land devoid of high culture. As Philip Drew wrote in his architectural study of the Sydney Opera House, the traditional image is contrary to the facts: '... more people in Australia visit art galleries and attend concerts than go to sports events'; it is also a fact that Australians purchase more books and magazine per capita than most other English-language countries. In fact, Drew goes on to say, such was the spirit of postwar yearning for change and cultural improvement in the Australia of the 1950s that 'only in Australia could anything so daring as Jørn Utzon's Opera House have been attempted'. Whether or not this is true, it is a fact that this daring break with tradition was accomplished in Australia, against numerous nay-sayers and traditionalists, against rampant criticism, and in spite of more difficulties than anyone could have foreseen.

Some facts

Under the shell roofs and within the massive podium are:

The Concert Hall, seating 2679
The Opera Theatre, seating 1547
The Drama Theatre, seating 544
The Playhouse, seating 398
The Studio, seating between 220 and 324
5 rehearsal studios
60 dressing rooms
5 restaurants
6 theatre bars
5 foyer and lounge areas
The 'Green Room' for performers and staff

Areas not open to the public include scenery docks, administration offices, kitchens, pantries, cold-rooms, laundries, wardrobe and wig rooms, and two vast areas underground housing the air-conditioning, electricals and security operations. Since 1993 there has also been a 1,100-space car park winding below the huge complex. The entire building occupies around 1.82 hectares (4.5 acres) of its 2.23 hectare (5.5 acre) site.

In all, there are 800 separate areas and 2,200 doors. The building is 183 metres (600 feet) long and, at its widest point, 118 metres

Photo: Courtesy of M.R. Hornibrook Pty Ltd

(388 feet) wide. Its foundations are concrete and its structure is of reinforced concrete. The highest roof is 67.4 metres (222 feet) above sea level, and its shell roofs, with an area of 18,500 square metres (199,030 square feet) are covered with 1.056 million glossy white and matt cream Swedish-made tiles. The glass windows use over 6223 square metres (66,971 square feet) of glass.

The Opera House is managed by the Sydney Opera House Trust. This was established in 1961, although the number of members was reduced and the committee reconstituted by new legislation enacted in early 1969. Its chief executive is the general manager of the Opera House. The Trust manages a complex operation: as well as hiring out the halls to major and minor users, it attempts to ensure that there is a range of attractions featured at any one time; that there are low-cost options and entertainment for children.

The House is open for nearly 16 hours a day, every day of the year except Christmas Day and Good Friday. There is someone on duty at all times, every day.

The performing spaces

The Concert Hall, with its suspended acoustic rings, moulded plywood ceilings and walls, and great organ. (Photo: Courtesy of M. R. Hornibrook Pty Ltd.)

The Concert Hall

As the largest performing area in the Opera House, the Concert Hall is used for a range of performances, from symphony concerts, chamber music, and dance, to rock and jazz concerts and miscellaneous uses such as conventions or public talks. The acoustics are well regarded by international critics. Adjustable acoustic rings, made from acrylic, are suspended directly above the stage. They help to reflect sound back to the stage so that performers can hear themselves.

The woods used in the Concert Hall are white birch plywood, which panels the ceiling and upper walls, and brush box, which is used on the lower walls, stairs, boxes and platform. The chairs are white birch, upholstered in magenta wool.

The Opera Theatre

This hall is used for opera, ballet and other dance performances. It is also panelled in wood, but the wood has been stained black on the ceiling and walls. The proscenium opening is 12 metres (39 feet) wide and 7 metres (23 feet) high and the stage is 25 metres (82 feet) deep. The stage floor incorporates a revolve of 14 metres (46 feet) in diameter and there are four platform lifts 10.5 metres by 3.5 metres (35 feet by 12 feet). These raise and lower the scenery between the stage and the set storage level below.

The orchestral pit seats around 80 musicians and can be raised to stage level for additional forestage space when required.

The carpet is a brilliant red and the seats are constructed from silver birch plywood. They were once upholstered with red leather, but years later, the leather was replaced with red wool.

The stage curtain is a famous tapestry designed by Australian John Coburn and woven by Aubusson in France using Australian wool. The bright abstract work is called *Curtain of the Sun*.

The Drama Theatre

This theatre is used for drama and dance. The walls are painted black, and the low ceiling is surfaced with refrigerated aluminium panels that moderate the temperature without noisy draughts. The 15-metre-long stage (49 feet) contains two revolves, one within the other. The proscenium height is 5 metres (16 feet) and

its width 15 metres (49 feet). The forestage area can be lowered to create an orchestra pit for 35 musicians.

The carpet is vivid blue and the seats covered with a striking vermilion wool. The stage curtain is the *Curtain of the Moon*, the companion piece to the curtain in the Opera Theatre. Woven in cooler colours, it is another abstract work by John Coburn.

The Playhouse

Once called The Music Room, this theatre is used principally for drama, lectures, seminars and movies, and is panelled with

Curtain of the Sun *by John Coburn is the* Opera Theatre curtain. (Photo: Courtesy of Australian Tourist Commission)

white birch plywood. The carpet is red, and the seats covered in charcoal-coloured wool. Originally it was used for chamber music, but as chamber music became more popular, it was moved to the more spacious Concert Hall. Sharp-eyed visitors will note that the rows of seats start with 'B', not 'A' — the result of removing one row of seats to make room for the larger stage required by theatre.

The Studio

The space presently occupied by the Studio, which opened in February 1999, has been put to a variety of uses. Much of it was originally the Recording Hall. The Recording Hall became the Broadwalk Studio, incorporating the Dennis Wolanski Library. Then it was refurbished to become the present Studio. It is the smallest and most intimate theatre in the complex, seating between 220 and 324 people 'in the round'. It was designed by Leif Kristensen, and cost $7.5 million. With red carpets and a predominant theme of wood finishings, it is used for contemporary music, comedy, cabaret and seminars.

The Drama Theatre, the Playhouse and the Studio, since 1999, share a large foyer

What's in a name?

Visitors often inquire as to why the building is known as the 'Sydney Opera House' since clearly it is a centre for all of the performing arts. Many different names were put forward regularly during its construction: Arts Centre, National Festival House, Harbour Hall and many others. Regularly, headlines proclaimed the possibility of another name being chosen. After the death of Premier Cahill, who had presided over and initiated government support for its construction, some people suggested that it be named after him. But he himself wanted it to be called Sydney Opera House, and since the idea for it came from Sydney's need for an opera house, and because that was its popular name throughout its years of construction, the name remained.

The open house

Today the Opera House is the busiest performing arts centre in the world. Over 200,000 visitors take guided tours of the Opera House every year, and around two million visit it for performances. Over 2000 events are staged there each year, and on any one evening there will be an average of 4000 people enjoying performances. There are concerts, operas, plays and any number of other entertainments — some free and set in the sunny outside areas on the harbour. Visitors can dine in excellent restaurants with spectacular views, take a moonlit walk around the extensive promenade, or even hire a foyer in which to get married. Foyer and reception areas can be booked for all manner of private functions. Most halls have convention facilities that include multilingual translation systems and film, PC or slide projection facilities.

which has given this side of the building a feeling of spaciousness that had been lacking when the Drama Theatre and the Playhouse had their own foyers.

Other non-performing spaces

The Green Room

This room, open to performers, staff and their invited guests, extends above the central passageway but below the major theatres. It incorporates a canteen used by performers, a bar and a spacious lounge looking out onto the harbour.

It's a pity this area is not accessible to the public as it presents some of the most philosophically and visually interesting sights in the building. It is not unusual to see a table of Egyptian slaves taking coffee between a group of tuxedo-clad musicians and assorted lairds and witches en route to and from Dunsinane.

The stage managers' announcements are heard here, and there are a number of closed-circuit televisions covering all the performances and rehearsals in progress. This is not an unmitigated blessing; one

The Restaurants

There are five restaurants including the Bennelong, probably the most well known and the one housed in its own shell. The Harbour offers outdoor tables in a relaxed, casual atmosphere on the water's edge at the front of the House. The Concourse Cafe and Bar, on the lower concourse, offers drinks and cafe style meals, while the Cafe Mozart, on the steps of the Concert Hall, serves light refreshments. The Espresso Bar sells coffee and light meals to take out and enjoy on the forecourt. On top of all this there are six theatre bars around the House offering drinks, coffee and snacks to patrons.

Shops and Markets

The Sydney Opera House Foyer Shop, the Aboriginal Artists Gallery, The Shop: Sydney Opera House, The Performing Arts Shop, the Opal Centre and Scribbly Graphics are all open within the Opera House building. A weekly Sunday market on the forecourt and promenades displays work by artists and artisans in around 40 stalls.

With the city skyline stretching out to its right and the glistening harbour before it, the Opera House forms the artistic hub

The Australian Youth Orchestra performing in the foyer. Carpeted in a royal purple, the back drop (not seen here) is John Olsen's Five Bells on one side and dazzling views of the Pacific Ocean through the glass walls on the other side. (Photo: Grenville Turner, Wildlight)

actor came desperately close to missing an entrance in *Arsenic and Old Lace* through becoming engrossed in watching *Rigoletto* on the monitor.

The Foyers

The foyers, with their glass walls and roofs, afford unparalleled views across the harbour and of the Sydney Harbour Bridge. They are furnished with bars which cater to patrons during performances, and they are used as informal spaces for children's concerts, book launches, fashion parades and receptions.

of the city. Long before it was built, its architect envisaged it as a 'white, shimmering thing — as alive to the eyes as architecture can make anything set in the blue-green waters of the Harbour'. Today it is hard to imagine that at one time the state of New South Wales was deeply divided over its design, construction and cost, and that from 1959 to 1973 it was the subject of frequent and vehemently poisonous debates in State Parliament, also known locally as the snake pit. There must be many people still alive today who would prefer not to remember their criticisms and forebodings of doom — such as the correspondent to the *Sydney Morning Herald* who declared that should 'our descendants regain any sense of taste or proportion, they will be forced to foot the bill for removing it and putting up something less repellent'. However, there are countless others, worldwide, who can remember their excitement that such a pioneering work of imagination would be built, and who voiced their support throughout the various controversies. Whatever happened in the past, one thing is clear today — the Opera House is almost universally praised and admired. It would be difficult to find serious critics

of its design, although there are many who lament that the interiors were not completed according to the designs of its creator, Jørn Utzon. To understand why they were not, it is necessary to turn to the story of the stormy years of construction.

The busy Concourse Cafe and Bar is a popular spot for a pre-show dinner. (Photo: Julia Collingwood)

'It is a dream that never was, a structure that could barely be built, an architectural tour de force, a politician's nightmare, a population's talking point, and much more.'

Sir Ove Arup and Jack Kunz

In the Beginning

When the decision to build an opera house for Sydney was taken, no one could have foreseen what was in store for the state. The road ahead was to be a long and difficult one, littered with controversy, great design and engineering challenges, and higher costs than anyone had ever dreamed.

The delays and mounting costs were a constant feature of the national news, and the tension between artistic perfection and cost considerations led ultimately to the resignation of the Opera House's brilliant architect. Utzon was never able to complete the interior of the building, but, by the time he left the country, never to return, the exterior had already attracted the esteem of architects and engineers worldwide. Today, of course, no one complains about the cost, but during its construction, it was a constant theme in public debate. The story of its creation is a fascinating

The City of Sydney by M.S. Hill. Painted in 1888, this picture shows the well-established Royal Botanic Gardens, Hyde Park, and Sydney as a busy port to both sailing and steam ships. (Reproduced courtesy of National Library of Australia)

human drama in which artistic vision clashes with pragmatism and politics. Like all such dramas, it is a story with both shameful and inspirational chapters.

Sydney in the 1950s was a growing city. Immigrants from Europe, fleeing depressed economies and the ravages of war, flocked to the 'land of opportunity and sunshine'. Many British arrived, as well as Italians, Greeks, Dutch, Germans and Hungarians.

The new immigrants added immeasurably to the vibrancy of the city, bringing new foods, new customs, and many European cultural expectations. There was an increased demand for all types of entertainment — the cinema, popular music, books and magazines. The growth in high culture, influenced partly by Jewish immigrants, was part of this cultural boom. Sydney began to hunger for a diet of music, opera, ballet and drama, and with this upsurge in artistic activity came the need for suitable venues. The city was the perfect location for a new arts centre: it had a burgeoning population, a growing economy, and an optimistic outlook.

In 1947, Eugene Goossens arrived in Australia. He was a highly regarded English composer who had been enticed to Sydney in order to take up the position of Chief Conductor of the Sydney Symphony Orchestra and as Director of the New South Wales State Conservatorium of Music.

Goossens was appalled that Sydney had no opera house, and immediately began to lobby for one, making vigorous representations to Charles Moses (later Sir Charles, then Director of the Australian Broadcasting Commission) and lobbying the press. A passionate egalitarian, he wanted music to be available to everyone, and for that, large auditoriums

North View of Sydney *is a charming 1824 hand-coloured aquatint by convict-artist Joseph Lycett. It clearly shows Fort Macquarie on Bennelong Point at the far left of the picture. (Reproduced courtesy of Josef Lebovic Gallery)*

were required. Architectural schools began to set designs for an opera house as exercises for students. The discussion had entered the public domain.

The Premier of New South Wales in 1952 was the Labor Party's John Joseph Cahill, and Moses arranged for Goossens to meet him. At that meeting, Cahill agreed that Sydney did indeed need a performance centre. From then on, he was deeply committed to the project, championing it against his sometimes reluctant colleagues.

The Site

The site was chosen by a committee that included Goossens, Moses, the architect Henry Ingham Ashworth, Stan Haviland,

the Under Secretary of the Department of Local Government, and a few others. Out of a number of proposed sites, they settled on Bennelong Point.

Premier Cahill accepted the idea, and then had to overcome objections from the Maritime Services Board and the Transport Department, both of which had designs on the site. On 17 May 1955, the choice was announced, to popular acclaim. Eero Saarinen, a judge in the ensuring architectural competition, called it 'one of the best sites for the purpose in the world'. It had Farm Cove to one side and Sydney Cove to the other: behind it lay the verdant stretch of Sydney's Botanical Gardens, and

before it all the drama of the harbour, with its expanses of blue water and its picturesque coves and inlets.

This small peninsula had been called Jubgalee by a local Aboriginal clan, the Cadigal. The harbour, with its plentiful fish and game, was populated by several clans speaking different languages. When the First Fleet arrived in 1788, the advance ship, *HMS Supply*, anchored there, in what Governor Phillip described as 'the finest harbour in the world'. Because cattle and horses from the ships were pastured there, early settlers called the area Cattle Point. It was separated from the mainland by a shallow stream, which was gradually filled in with rubble.

Later, it was named after Bennelong, an Aboriginal who had served as a liaison between the British and the Aboriginal people. He was an intelligent and intrepid character who was known for the skill with which he would imitate various Europeans — especially a French cook. Governor Phillip built him a house on the point and later Bennelong accompanied him to England, returning two years later.

By this stage the European occupation of the harbour had already brought tragedy for the Aboriginal people: half of

'One of the best sites for the purpose in the world', said one of the judges: but in 1958 Bennelong Point was just a bus station. (Courtesy of Max Dupain and Associates Pty Ltd)

them had died of smallpox. In spite of Governor Phillip's relatively enlightened views, the Aboriginal population of the harbour area was gradually decimated or displaced. The rich harbour area must have been an ideal home for its Aboriginal inhabitants. But a fundamental disdain for indigenous peoples characterised the age of European colonisation and, consequently, their lands were appropriated freely and without compensation. As visitors gaze out on the bustling harbour, it is hard to imagine it in its pristine state, and to comprehend what

a great tragedy was suffered by the Aboriginal people in its loss.

The colony continued to grow apace. A saltworks was established on the site in 1795, and in 1796, Bennelong's house was pulled down. Fortunately, the early governors established this foreshore area as Crown land. Fort Macquarie, designed by the famous convict architect Francis Greenway, was erected on the spot in 1817. In 1902 the Fort was incorporated into a larger structure to become a tram depot, and rubble was used to extend the site

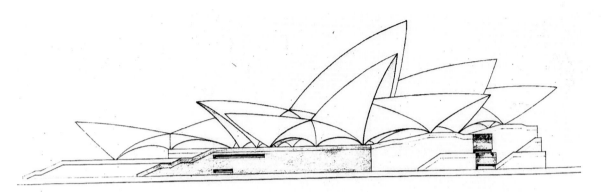

into the harbour. The 'picnic jetties' were built and ferries docked there to pick up passengers for excursions. One can imagine it as a popular site — a place to enjoy the lovely harbour, to meet friends and to embark on myriad journeys. However, it did not meet with the aesthetic appreciation of everyone. John Yeomans, in his book *The Other Taj Mahal*, remembers it as 'a hideous brick box with little turrets and battlements ... concealing a swarm of the hellish vehicles which clanged and lurched over the Sydney metropolitan area'.

In 1956 the tram depot was converted to a bus station, and finally, in late 1958, destroyed to make way for the Opera House. Today it is almost impossible to imagine Bennelong Point as a bus station, or as the location for any other prosaic function. Its inspiring view, prominence, and centrality make it the perfect site for an important building.

An International Competition

Once the site was chosen, a design was the next priority. A committee made up of Moses, Goossens, and several others drew up the conditions of entry for an international design competition which was advertised worldwide. It opened in February 1956 and closed in December 1956. The conditions were set out in 'The Brown Book'. In this booklet were 11 large pictures of the site, the building requirements, and the weather conditions in Sydney, such as wind speed. The stated requirements were for two halls, one seating 3000–3500, and a smaller one seating 1200, plus provision for a large organ,

rehearsal rooms, a broadcasting centre, a restaurant, meeting rooms, foyers and amenities.

An international panel of judges was made up of Henry Ingham Ashworth, Professor of Architecture at the University of Sydney and who was the chairman of the panel; Leslie Martin, Professor of Architecture at the University of Cambridge; Cobden Parkes, the New South Wales Government Architect; and Eero Saarinen, a Finnish-born US architect renowned for contemporary design. Interestingly, Saarinen's architect father had entered a previous competition in Australia — the one to design Canberra City — and had come second.

Two-hundred and thirty-three* entries from about 33 countries were submitted, 61 from Australian architects. The judges laboured over their task in an upstairs room in the Art Gallery of New South Wales. Finally, the day of the decision arrived. On 29 January 1957, after infuriating the audience by delaying the announcement until the end of a long speech, Premier Cahill announced the result. The winning design was No. 218, by Jørn Utzon, a 38-year-old Danish architect.

When a reporter managed to get through to Utzon's home, he was taking a walk. His daughter Lin, then just 10 years old, cycled hurriedly into the woods, alarming Utzon who feared that something had gone awry at home. But her news was good news — he had won the competition for the Sydney Opera House! The little girl demanded on the spot that her father finally buy her the horse she wanted.

*Varying accounts of the number of entries exist: from 217 to 233, depending on whose account you read.

Although Utzon's sketches were the least 'finished' of the finalist's designs, the judges were so impressed with the design that it was chosen unanimously. A story persists that Saarinen had been unavailable for the first 11 days of judging, and on his arrival, he was shown 10 designs that the others had chosen. He didn't like any of them, and flicking through the remaining designs, he found Utzon's drawing. Presenting it to his colleagues, he said 'Gentlemen, this is the first prize'. Professor Ashworth claimed that this was untrue, saying that Saarinen was there for most of the judging, and that Utzon's design was always one of the top choices. Whatever the truth, it is usually recognised that Saarinen did champion the building and insisted, against some objections, that it could be built. For this, Sydney owes the late Saarinen a great debt.

The second prize went to a group of six Philadelphia architects headed by J. Marzella; the third prize to Bossevain & Osmond, of London. Both were respectable entries, but neither displayed the vision and inventiveness of the Utzon design. Ironically, in light of the later controversies about the cost of the building, the judges announced that both of the runner-up designs would have cost significantly more than Utzon's design. Understandably, no one realised that the building would require such advanced engineering techniques and would pose so many challenges.

On awarding the prize, the judges said: 'The drawings submitted are simple to the point of being diagrammatic ... nevertheless we have returned again and again to the study of these drawings. We are convinced that they present a concept of an opera house which is capable of being one of the great buildings of the world. We consider this scheme to be the most original and creative submission. Because of its very originality it is clearly a controversial design. We are, however, absolutely convinced about its merits.'

The building that Utzon envisaged was to be set on a massive pedestal and would incorporate a vast open stairway. The shells would rise from the ground and curve towards a ridge. It was, as the architect Harry Seidler put it, 'pure poetry'. The design allowed for two halls side-by-side, both facing the harbour and taking advantage of the spectacular setting. The podium, designed to surround the halls, allowed for quick egress in an emergency and eliminated the need for fire escapes. The drama of the design, with its 'magnificent

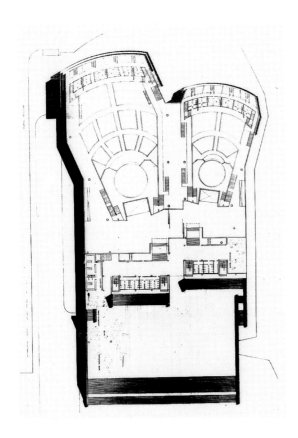

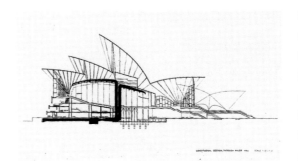

ceremonial approach' and auditoriums arranged 'like Greek theatres' also caught the imagination of the panel.

However, even at this early stage, dissenting voices were heard. Letters to the city newspapers described the design as looking like 'an insect with a shell on its back', 'a gargantuan monster', and 'a monument to the clever ugliness of modernness'.

Others forecast that it would be a 'constant eyesore'. The design was simply too revolutionary to find universal favour. But hundreds of letters praised it: it was 'refreshing', 'stimulating', 'a piece of poetry' and 'a large and lovely ship of the imagination'. Overseas, both praise and condemnation were heard. Surprisingly, given Utzon's admiration for his architecture, Frank Lloyd Wright was one of the more strident critics, calling it a 'reckless design' and 'sensationalism'.

Jørn Utzon

Utzon was a 38-year-old Danish architect, tall and handsome, with a ready smile. When he arrived in Sydney (flying tourist class, to the amazement of reporters) in July 1957 he was an immediate hit with the media. Although relatively unknown,

he had already won a number of architectural awards. Utzon had worked under a number of notable architects, including Alvar Aalto, and was particularly interested in 'organic architecture': architecture that evoked and resembled natural forms. As Philip Drew wrote in his 1999 biography of Utzon, *Masterpiece*, Utzon 'regarded nature as the one great inspiration of the designer ... Natural processes were at once remarkably economical and efficient and chillingly beautiful'. In the Opera House, Utzon designed a building that brilliantly reflected both this economy and beauty. The shells rising from the podium evoke billowing sails or the wings of a bird in flight. Perched on the edge of the harbour and framing the passing cavalcade of sailboats and ships, the building is the perfect echo of its surrounds. Architectural writers enthuse about the abundance of organic themes: the tiles are described by Philip Drew in his architectual study of the Sydney Opera House as resembling 'great fish scales glistening in the sunlight' and the glass windows as 'a kind of glass waterfall'. Famously, Utzon drew inspiration from Kronborg Castle at Elsinore, in Denmark. 'There you have forms against a horizontal line like the sea or the clouds without a single vertical line, nothing constituting a weight, and forms that are different from all angles.' The influence of ancient architecture on Utzon, in particular Mayan platforms, gave rise to the idea of the podium.

Utzon was truly a modern architect, dedicated to industrial methods of construction using prefabrication. His solution to the problem of the shells, as we shall see, showed an ability to combine the beauty of free design with economical standardisation of elements. As Philip Drew wrote in the preface to *Masterpiece*, 'Utzon humanised and opened up Modernism to include ideas about organic form, without abandoning its commitment to standardisation or the industrialisation of the building process'.

Ove Arup and Partners

Utzon, in consultation with the Committee, had approved the appointment of Ove Arup and Partners Consulting Engineers, a highly respected firm based in London. Arup was an energetic and likable man. He greatly admired the design, calling it the 'most marvellous building of the century'. He foresaw the difficulties but was determined to support Utzon, whom he deeply liked, in finding solutions. 'It was an adventure into the unknown. In the early days we were told it would be a miracle to get it to work. We did our utmost to achieve that miracle.'

In March 1958 Utzon, along with Ove Arup, returned to Australia, and presented the government with the *Red Book,* showing photographs of his preliminary models. He had begun to grapple with the structural constraints of his designs. His brief had changed slightly — the government now wanted four theatres rather than just two. Control of the project was placed under the newly formed Opera House Committee, under the leadership of Mr Stan Haviland, the permanent head of the Department of Local Government.

Now worn and weathered with age, the Red Book *— presented to the government by Utzon — is part of the archival material held at the Mitchell Library in Sydney. It contains drawings and plans for the Opera House during the heady early days of planning. (Courtesy of Mitchell Library, State Library of NSW)*

'It is not so much a building
as a controversy.'

Sir Ove Arup and Jack Zunz

Construction Begins

The construction of the foundations began on 2 March 1959, just after a plaque-laying ceremony. Premier Cahill's speech was optimistic and enthusiastic. 'I am glad to say that the Opera House is purely non-political and I venture to predict that no party will attempt to make an issue of it in the coming election.' Little did he know that in six years the Labor Government would fall because of the Opera House.

The government was not legally bound to go ahead with the building after selecting the winner: it was only required to pay the £5000 prize. In fact, in the first year after the competition, there were fears that the project might be dropped. Pressure groups within the Labor Party called for homes and hospitals to be built not an opera house, which some saw as an extravagant luxury. In the end, after many ominous headlines in June and July of 1957 forecasting a likely defeat of Cahill's project, the Labor Party Caucus voted conclusively to support the Opera House. It was a victory for Cahill, and for the entire nation.

Cahill had only a narrow majority in the caucus of the State Parliamentary Labor Party and he was facing a state election in just three weeks so, despite the designs being incomplete, he gave the order to start work on what was now his pet project. Fortunately for Cahill, and probably for the Opera House, the Labor Party survived the election with a five-seat majority. Utzon's design had been controversial and Cahill no doubt felt that he must push the project through while he still had the chance. It is fortunate that he did, because although this early start was later to have very expensive ramifications when some aspects of the foundation had to be changed, Cahill died only seven months later. If he had delayed, it is quite possible that the Opera House would never have been built.

So closely connected was Cahill to the project that for the first three years it was supervised by the New South Wales Premier's Department. After the passing of the *Sydney Opera House Act*, however, the more conventional overseeing body was the Department of Public Works, under three successive ministers: Pat Ryan (1960–1965, Labor), Davis Hughes (1965–1972, Country) and Leon Punch (1972–1973, Liberal). (Today the Sydney Opera House Trust reports to the New South Wales Parliament through the Minister for the Arts.)

In order to fund the construction without eating into money needed for schools, hospitals, and such like, a public appeal was launched. The Sydney Opera House Appeal Fund opened on 7 August 1957 and such was the enthusiastic response that £235,500, inaugurated with a hefty starting donation of £100,000 from the State Government, was raised within the first few hours. However, by December only £450,000 had been raised — far short of the projected £3.2 million. So, in 1958, the Opera House Lottery was started, with a prize of £100,000. Critics didn't think the amount could be raised, but the Opera House Lottery gave big prizes and Australians love to gamble. In the next 17 years, 496 lotteries were conducted, selling $297 million dollars worth of tickets. After prizes and running costs were deducted, $101 million was raised — very nearly the cost of the Sydney Opera House. Some questioned the morality of financing a public building by gambling, but a better way of raising the money without draining the state coffers could probably not have been found. As David Messent wrote in *Opera House Act One*, '... money poured into the Opera House account from the proceeds of the lotteries like manna from heaven. It was wonderful, like picking pound notes from a money tree, as if no one was having to pay for it'.

There was a tragic episode in the history of these lotteries. In 1960, the eight-year-old son of one of the winners, Basil Thorne, was kidnapped, held for ransom, and murdered. From that time on the names of the winners were only published with the permission of the ticket holder.

In October 1959, Premier Cahill collapsed in Parliament House during a caucus meeting and died a few days later. He had played a vital role in the inception of the Opera House, but would never see more than its earliest stages. Utzon often praised him for his support, as did many other participants in the drama of the construction. As Sir Charles Moses said in an interview with the *Sydney Morning Herald*, 'If ever a man deserved to have his name perpetuated in this building it is Joe Cahill'.

New South Wales Premier Joe Cahill fought tenaciously for an opera house against a lot of opposition, including from within his own Labor Party.

Left: The first Opera House Lottery ticket. (Courtesy of New South Wales Lotteries)

Bottom left: The cover of the Yellow Book, now discoloured, was presented to the government in 1962 and shows Utzon's ingenious spherical solution to the problem of shell design. (Courtesy of Mitchell Library, State Library NSW)

The Controversy Starts

As construction began, Premier Cahill had announced that the cost of the building would be around $7.2 million dollars. But the cost was already blowing out. By the next year, the figure was up to $9.8 million. Similarly, the completion date, originally scheduled for December 1963, would be deferred over and over again.

Construction was planned in three stages: Stage I was to be the foundations and podium; Stage II the roofs; and Stage III the interiors. In 1962, as Stage I was being finished, Utzon, with the backing of the civil engineer, Ove Arup, announced new plans for the roofs. After years of wrestling with the problem, he had come up with an ingenious solution for the roofs, but it meant that the pillars in the foundation were no longer strong enough to support the new, heavier roofs. New plans also meant new drawings and new calculations. The *Yellow Book*, showing the new roof designs and the preliminary interior designs, was presented to the government in early 1962.

> Utzon was a perfectionist. He wanted the Opera House to be the best it could possibly be ... He would not allow anything that did not meet his exacting standards to pass.

In 1963, construction of the roofs began, and around the same time, Utzon, with his wife and three children, arrived to live in Sydney. He continued to devote himself to the Opera House, grappling with the challenges that his unique design created.

During these years, headlines proclaimed each new cost estimate: in 1964 the latest estimate was $35 million, about five times the initial estimate. Letters to local newspapers either poured vitriol on the whole project or staunchly defended it. Newspaper editorials opined that the project would have never been started had the citizens been aware of the true cost. The project was also bedevilled by strikes, go-slows and stop-work meetings. It was the 1960s and there was virtually full employment in Sydney, so campaigns for better wages and conditions were in full swing.

Utzon was a perfectionist. He wanted the Opera House to be the best it could possibly be, and it was said more than once that Utzon would never accept any solution to a problem if there was a better solution to be had. He would not allow anything that did not meet his exacting standards to pass.

Storm clouds were gathering. The government's concern at the cost was at odds with Utzon's focus on the aesthetics of the most important building ever built in Australia. Another state election was approaching, and the Liberal-Country Party Opposition was baying for blood, trumpeting that Labor had mismanaged the Opera House. Its election strategy was to promise an efficient and speedy completion of the project, and to increase public annoyance over a project that never seemed to get any closer to completion and yet swallowed more and more money. Even Utzon's fees became an issue, although they were not exorbitant, and the public was quick to forget that he paid his entire staff out of his fees.

In 1965 the Labor Party was defeated at the polls. The newly installed Liberal-Country Party coalition government under Premier Askin immediately began to exercise more control over costs. Davis Hughes of the Country Party, and Minister for Public Works, summoned Utzon to his office and berated him about missed deadlines and growing costs. Utzon was now forced to report personally to the Minister on costs and on his own fees. The government's treatment of this brilliant architect took on the character of errant schoolboy-style discipline. With some of his fees withheld and his own staff awaiting payment, Utzon, who had devoted himself to achieving the best solutions to the challenges of design, was frustrated. The continued conflict between him, an uncompromising artist, and Hughes, the politician, resulted in Utzon's resigning during a meeting on 26 February 1966. Two days later he confirmed his resignation in writing, citing the withholding of fees, the lack of collaboration and lack of respect for him as the architect. His resignation was quickly accepted, demonstrating how strained relations had become — and, perhaps, how little the new government valued Utzon's contribution.

A storm of protest erupted as soon as the resignation was made public. In spite of demonstrations in the street, pressure from architectural circles and the parliamentary Opposition, and a great deal of condemnation in the press, talks between Utzon and Hughes failed to produce a reconciliation. Utzon was offered a post as 'design architect' reporting to the government's architect, who would be in charge. This untenable solution was rejected by Utzon, who made counter-proposals, offering to work closely with a panel of architects. His

> Storm clouds were gathering. The government's concern at the cost was at odds with Utzon's focus on the aesthetics of the most important building ever built in Australia.

suggestions were rejected. Hughes further inflamed feelings by announcing that under Utzon, the Opera House 'would never be finished'.

Letters to the paper and editorials expressed outrage at the government's intransigence. Calls from many architects to boycott the project in support of Utzon divided the architectural community. The architect Harry Seidler formed the 'Utzon-in-Charge' committee which organised international petitions from noted architects. Sir Charles Moses spoke sadly of the resignation. He greatly admired Utzon's willingness to try to meet all the demands of his clients. Moses related that on one occasion, Utzon had spent a great deal of time working on a particular design requirement that was later scrapped. Instead of expressing annoyance, Utzon immediately began to work on a new design, saying to Moses: 'Architecture is a very exciting art. Always there are problems, and for every problem there is a solution. For me, it's exciting to find solutions to problems'.

Utzon left Australia in the same month that the last rib was raised into place. As one headline expressed it, the architect's dream had turned into a nightmare. The 'beautiful, white, shimmering thing', as he once described his vision, was never to be seen by him. The fact that his departure in no way signalled an end to cost blow-outs or delays is one of the saga's great ironies. In fact, much more money was spent after Utzon left, and the project was subject to extensive delays. Instead of the praise and gratitude he should have received, Utzon was subject to the vilest suggestions of self-interest and incompetence.

A New Team of Architects is Appointed

The government appointed a team of four architects to complete the job. E.H. Farmer, the New South Wales Government Architect, was to represent the government. Peter Hall, the youngest of the group and an award-winning architect, was given responsibility for design. Lionel Todd was responsible for contract documents and David Littlemore was responsible for the day-to-day supervision of construction. M.R. Hornibrook Pty Ltd, the construction firm engaged on Stage II, was engaged to complete the job in Stage III.

These architects had before them a most unenviable task. They were charged

Opposite: The completed building. Tragically, Utzon was never to see his masterpiece in its finished state. (Photo: Anne Fraser.)

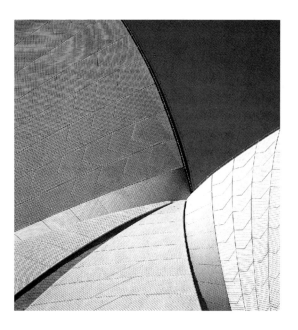

Utzon designed the Opera House as he would a sculpture; to be viewed from all sides. (Courtesy of M.R. Hornibrook Pty Ltd)

with finishing a work of art that had become embroiled in controversy. They might face criticism for any changes they made to the original designs, and vilification for accepting the commission at all. Furthermore, the requirements for the major halls were changing. The architects had before them demands from the Australian Broadcasting Commission (ABC) that the reverberation for the major hall should be suitable for orchestral concerts and be at least two seconds in duration, and this differed from the reverberations that opera required. To solve this and other problems, Hall, Todd and Littlemore, after a great deal of research and planning, proposed major changes to the interior design in a submission to Hughes on 12 December 1966 entitled 'Review of Program'.

Bitter controversy erupted again when these changes became known. The principal element of the rethink involved changing the major hall to a dedicated concert hall. Opera was to take place in the smaller hall. The ABC, which had lobbied for this change, was happy; the Elizabethan Theatre Trust (which ran the Australian Opera) was not. Dr H. C. Coombs, chairperson of the Elizabethan Theatre Trust, did his best to counter the proposal. The Sydney Opera House Trust also supported the idea of a dual-purpose hall, as did Sir Charles Moses, the ABC's former general manager.

Utzon, when approached by the *Australian* newspaper in February 1968, said he had worked out the dual-purpose solution and offered to come back under 'mutually acceptable terms', but the government refused to invite him. Many influential people and press articles urged the government seriously to attempt reconciliation again. These appeals fell on deaf ears. The government had approved the 'Review of Program' in March 1967, and work commenced on Stage III.

The changes caused long delays and more structural work. A huge steel stage tower for opera, already built, was scrapped and the stage concreted over. The area under the stage, originally allocated for scene-changing machinery and now no longer needed, was converted into a recording and rehearsal studio. Sam Hoare of Hornibrooks called it 'the biggest alteration job I've ever done'.

Stage III took from 1967 to July 1973. There are still critics of the final design of the interior. However, many have praised the design work of Peter Hall, who worked with the entire team under invidious circumstances, and there is no doubt that they attempted to fulfil Utzon's vision as well as going some way to satisfying the demands of the major users. Controversy continues to wax and wane over the integrity of the interiors, and most commentators lament the fact that Utzon was not able to finish the building. But whatever the reservations about the interior, the final result is a beautiful building which has far surpassed many of the original expectations. It is an iconic image, a very busy performance centre, an architectural wonder and an engineering feat all in one.

With hindsight, it is clear that several more years of planning in the initial stages of the project would have saved the government a great deal of money. Yet who is to know whether the project would have gone ahead had the full cost and the construction time required been known from the start? It is quite possible that the whole project would have been shelved by a government sensitive to public concerns about frivolous spending, or that it would have fallen victim to political point-scoring. As it is, Sydney — and the cause of progressive architecture — can be thankful that the Opera House was successfully built. It now stands as a monument to Jørn Utzon: despite his departure, the Opera House, in the words of Françoise Fromonot, 'embodies the intentions of his youth ... it was with this building that his universe of ideas and forms was crystallised in the most striking way'. It is his masterpiece, the building that became an icon, an emblem of modernity, and a symbol of a country.

> The Opera House 'embodies the intentions of his youth ... it was with this building that his universe of ideas and forms was crystallised in the most striking way'.
> *Françoise Fromonot*

Over: The Sydney Opera House with Sydney's other famous landmark, the Sydney Harbour Bridge. (Photo: Anne Fraser)

'Architecture is a very exciting art. Always there are problems, and for every problem there is a solution. For me, it's exciting to find solutions to problems.'

Jørn Utzon, to Sir Charles Moses, quoted in the Sydney Morning Herald *15 October 1973*

An Adventure into the Unknown

The Opera House design was supremely modern, and highly experimental. Building it was 'an adventure into the unknown', said Sir Ove Arup, the consultant engineer. No such edifice had ever been built before, and with hindsight it is clear that it was bound to require extensive design time. An engineer from Ove Arup's firm recalled that: 'This was the kind of building we could have worked on for 10 years and we didn't get half-a-year before the foundations went in'. Due to the pressures detailed in the previous chapter, the building was designed as it was built — on the job. Construction firms were engaged stage by stage and throughout, Ove Arup and Partners, based in London, acted as consultant engineers. Utzon himself employed a staff of around 15 architects and other assistants. Numerous specialist consultants were engaged to deal with acoustics, lighting, airconditioning and computing, to name but a few aspects of the job. As well, there were thousands of tradesmen and labourers working on the site — around 8000 during the whole project, with around 1500 persons on the site at any one time. During construction, there was only one fatal accident — a remarkable record for such a large project.

Stage I: 1959–1963

Foundations and Podium

Civil & Civic Pty Ltd was one of six firms invited to tender for the first stage of construction — the foundations and podium. Its tender was the lowest, at £1,397,929, and the contract was signed on 5 February 1959. It was an enormous job, made more complicated by the fact that finished plans were not yet fully available. Stage I took four years, and more than two years were spent on the foundations.

The Opera House site is surrounded on three sides by sea walls of big sandstone blocks. Within the enclosed area lies fill of varying depth and substance; below the fill lies Hawkesbury sandstone, interlaced with clay seams and ironstone bands. Water permeates the fill easily. Because the podium extends on the eastern side over the original sea wall, and because the rock drops sharply around the entire length of the perimeter, about 700 bored concrete piers were built to support the Opera House, each of them nearly a metre (around 3 feet) in diameter. These concrete piers were lined with steel casing. In the centre of the site, conventional reinforced concrete foundations rest on 'strip' or 'pad' form footings, used to replace fill and unstable rock.

Once the foundations were in place, the great podium began to appear. Utzon explained that his massive platform was inspired by Aztec and Mayan architecture: 'The platform as an architectural element is a fascinating feature. I first fell in love with it in Mexico on a study trip in 1949 … It's a tremendous experience to see how an architectural idea must have evolved in order to create contact with the gods'. Utzon was fascinated with the way the platform lifted the viewer out of the encroaching jungle: the vast, processional steps were a sort of metaphor for elevating people into the world of imagination

The podium under construction: it is 95.2 metres (313 feet) wide, 183 metres (602 feet) long, and is surrounded by a wide promenade on three sides. (Reproduced with permission from the Mitchell Library, State Library of NSW)

and culture. When the writer Patrick White visited it, he wrote to a friend that as he walked up the monumental steps, he 'kept thinking of Phaestos, Mycenae and Tyrins'. 'At last', he wrote, 'we are going to have something worth having'. (Quoted from *Patrick White: Letters,* edited by David Marr.)

The podium is a huge building constructed in reinforced concrete. It covers 1.62 hectares (four acres) and has 152,500 square metres (500,000 square feet) of floor space on three levels. The platform is reached by steps stretching over 91.5 metres (300 feet), one of the biggest open stairways in the world. Within the structure, there were to be dressing rooms, canteens, restaurants, wig and wardrobe rooms, storage rooms, offices, set areas, workshops, airconditioning plant rooms — around 900 rooms in all.

In February 1963, Stage I was finished. By then, intensive design work on Stage II had occupied Utzon and Ove Arup's firm for years.

Stage II (1963–1967)

The Exteriors, Including the Roofs

Undoubtedly, the major challenge in the construction of the Opera House was in the distinctive shells that formed the roofs — the 'fifth façade', as Utzon liked to call them. The original designs showed freeform curvatures for each shell, a factor that meant individual construction of each. The architect planned to pour concrete into immense wooden frameworks supported by scaffolding. However, since no one knew whether the shells would be self-supporting, an enormous amount of preliminary research was required. The difficulties were compounded by the unique shape of each shell. Models of various shapes — parabaloids and then ellipsoids — were built and tested, with computers used extensively for the many geometrical calculations, but the complexity of the shapes made it immensely difficult to arrive at a solution. The final structure had to support the weight of the shells themselves, a significant part of the weight of the windows (as they were to be, in part, 'hung' from the shells), and the ceilings of the halls. Furthermore, they had to be capable of withstanding the highest winds ever likely to occur, plus a range of temperature variations — the shape meant that at times one side of the shells could be considerably hotter than the other side.

Utzon's ingenious spherical solution to the problem of building the shells meant that the ribs could be made from just a few moulds, as they followed the meridian curves on spheres of the same radius. (Courtesy of Ove Arup and Partners)

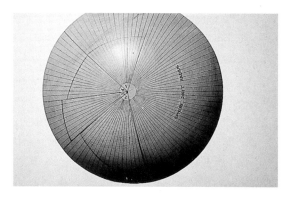

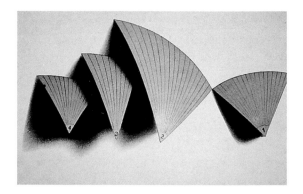

In October 1961, Utzon came up with an ingenious solution to construction of the shells. He redrew the shells so that each would fit on the outside of spheres with a common radius of about 80 metres, or about 246 feet. This breakthrough meant that the ribs could be constructed of unit blocks, cast on the site and then erected into position. The ribs were divided into segments following the meridian curves on spheres of the same radius.

The extraordinary difficulty of the problem is illustrated by the amount of time it took to do all the calculations and tests: Ove Arup, in a frank interview published in 1973 in the *Australian* newspaper, estimated his firm devoted around 700,000 hours and 150 people to the problem. This equates to one person working 40-hour weeks for 336 years. Utzon recognised all this in a gift he sent to colleagues for Christmas 1963. Instead of the traditional card, he sent 'an elegant white box in white cardboard on which was printed a series of interlaced red circles. It contained a cut-out puzzle of a photograph of the building site accompanied by the observation: "It took several hundred men some years to put this together. I am sure you can do it in an hour"'. (Quoted

from Françoise Fromonot's *Jørn Utzon: The Sydney Opera House*.)

The solution was one that would save a great deal of time and money. But the solution also meant that the engineers needed to perform many new calculations, and it also meant changes to the foundation, including blasting away and replacing

Three French-built cranes towered over the site as the ribs begin to take shape. (Photo: Max Dupain, courtesy of Max Dupain and Associates Pty Ltd)

The shell pedestals bristled with steel reinforcement. (Courtesy of Ove Arup and Partners)

the now inadequate supporting pillars. The Public Works Department now signed a contract for the Stage II construction with an Australian company, M.R. Hornibrook (New South Wales) Pty Ltd. Hornibrooks was run by Manuel Hornibrook, a man who thrived on challenges. His manager on the job was Corbet Gore, who said in one interview that the job they were taking on was 'the most fascinating engineering job in the world today'.

Each of the shells is constructed by twin opposing rows of ribs which curve up from the podium and meet at the centreline. Ten massive moulds shaped the ribs which were cast on site. Three French-built cranes, the biggest of their type in the world and costing $100,000 each, could lift the huge rib sections from anywhere in the site. The rib segments themselves were hollow, with a Y-shaped interior. To support them while they were being placed in position, four great steel erection arches were designed by Hornibrooks. Some of the ribs were 45.75 metres (150 feet) high and there were 2194 separate segments to make up 280 ribs of varying sizes, all weighing 26,800 tonnes. The segments were, surprisingly, glued together by an epoxy resin, a technique used in the United States for railway sleepers but never before in a building project. From the beginning, both Hornibrooks and Ove Arup and Partners had realised that the job was really at the outer limits of what was technically feasible. By careful design, and by the then largely unprecedented use of computers for the many calculations required, the two firms and Utzon surmounted the difficulties. The first segments were put into place on 22 November 1963.

John Yeomans, in his entertaining book *The Other Taj Mahal*, gives a good description of the placement of the ribs. He asks

By 1965 Sydney's ferry commuters could see the exciting forms of the Opera House taking shape. (Photo: Max Dupain, courtesy of Max Dupain and Associates Pty Ltd)

us to imagine that we are watching the construction of Rib 7 of Shell A2. Rib 6 East and West have already been erected.

The erection arch is so manipulated that it assumes exactly the curvature and future position of Rib 8, leaving a vacant space between the arch and Rib 6. In this space, the segments to make Rib 7 are lowered one at a time, starting, naturally, with the bottom segments which rest on a concrete pedestal previously built in situ. Now the crane lowers the new segment into the waiting space until the bottom is almost kissing the top of the segment laid just before it. The completed Rib 6 holds the new segment in place on one side, the erection arch holds it in place on the other and the ends of the needles on the new block stop it from falling right through and landing on

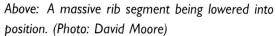

Above: A massive rib segment being lowered into position. (Photo: David Moore)

Top Right: The tile lids were formed, then hung, like laundry on a clothes line, to await positioning. (Photo: Max Dupain, courtesy of Max Dupain and Associates Pty Ltd)

Right: The exhilarating shape of the ribs and the interplay of light and shade made the new building seem like a modern cathedral to the arts. (Photo: Max Dupain, courtesy of Max Dupain and Associates Pty Ltd)

the floor inside the shell. When the block is only a few inches off its final resting place, the erection gang puts on the glue, which looks like condensed milk and is spread without fuss with a stick or an ordinary household paint roller. The block is then lowered to the one beneath it and stressed — that is, kept in place by the use of internal steel cables.

Once the rib was stressed, using nine steel cables, and its opposing rib was constructed and stressed, additional stressing cables were threaded up through both ribs and the crown piece, forming a stable arch.

The 'lids' were the final cladding. They were formed from curved chevron-shaped moulds in which concrete was poured; then the tiles were positioned on top of the wet concrete. Bolts were set into the rear of the lids. Then they were hung up, like laundry on a clothes-line, to await positioning. Lid placement started in February 1966 and was completed in March 1967. As placement of the 4220 curved panels demanded great accuracy, Hornibrooks again had to design its own techniques and slinging devices. Several trials were made before the best method of positioning the tiles was achieved; again computer calculations were essential.

The tiles were manufactured in Sweden especially to Utzon's requirements by a company called Hoganas. True to his exacting nature, he had been to China and Japan to find the right tiles, but finally had to commission them, and spent two years in close collaboration with Hoganas in order to develop the perfect tile. They are called 'self-cleaning tiles' because they are very non-porous, and so do not absorb dirt and are easily cleaned by rain. To avoid glare, Utzon had Hoganas design a slightly ribbed surface. They were formed in two colours: a glossy off-white and a matt cream colour. The matt cream-coloured tiles were used to outline each chevron mould, for the uppermost ridges, and to form patterns on the lower parts and smaller shells. The colour variance provides the distinct textural appeal of the shells and emphasises the different shapes.

The right tiles were absolutely vital to the impact that the building would make. In conversation with Sir Charles Moses, and quoted by David Messent in *Opera House Act One*, Utzon explained that he'd

'Interplay is so important that together with the sun, the light and the clouds, it makes a living thing ... When the sun shines, it gives an effect which varies in all these curved areas ...'

Utzon in 1965, talking about the tiles.

Even during construction, the Opera House was inspiring Australia's greatest painters.
Above: William Dobell's Opera House Sydney Harbour, 1968. (Copyright Sir William Dobell Art Foundation, reproduced courtesy of Portrait of Australia Collection, Foster's Brewing Group Ltd)

Lloyd Rees' Opera House from Kirribilli, *painted in 1966. (Reproduced courtesy of Alan and Jancis Rees)*

essence of the Opera House and illustrate how, when a complex thing is reduced to simplicity, the result can be an extraordinary grandeur'.

As the graceful ribs were rising heavenwards during Stage II, costs were also soaring. Wet weather, strikes and the new plans had contributed towards the blow-outs. Headlines were screaming about costs. The State Opposition was accusing the government of mismanagement. When the Liberal-Country Opposition came to power in 1965, its policies towards funding led to worsening relations between client and architect. In February 1966, placement of the tile lids was just beginning, and Utzon had been eager to see them in place. But in that same month, the conflict increased to such a level that Utzon resigned. A panel of architects, under the Government Architect Ted Farmer, was appointed to complete the job.

selected a mixture of matt and gloss tiles in order to achieve 'the colour you get on snowcapped mountains when the sun is setting: the beautiful pink and violet reflection from the combination of matt snow and shiny ice'. To Philip Drew, Utzon's biographer, the tiles are a revealing example of Utzon's approach to architecture. They 'encapsulate the

Above and top right: Two photographs by David Moore showing the tile lids being placed to form the outer skin of the Opera House; the workmen are dwarfed by the massive ribs.

Opposite and right: Two photographs by Max Dupain showing workmen clambering like mountain climbers over the steeply rising segments to finalise the placement of the tiles. (Courtesy of Max Dupain and Associates Pty Ltd)

'The concept, design and construction of the Sydney Opera House stand as an affirmation for twentieth century man - that by his imagination and by his own hand he can shape his world to his needs.'

Sir Ove Arup

The Interior Takes Shape

Utzon had been deeply involved in his plans for the final third stage: the interiors, the seating plans, and the acoustical ceilings. Now the panel of architects were commissioned to finish the building as quickly as possible. They retained the Stage II construction company, Hornibrooks, and put out for tender the contracts for supply of glass, paving, and the ceilings.

The spherical shape of the shells had changed the volumes of the halls, and problems with acoustics, large expanses of glass, the orchestra pit and seating remained. The acoustical suitability of the major hall was one of the concerns. The original specifications had been followed in Utzon's design, but, as described in Chapter 3, the prevailing opinion was that a dual-purpose hall, for both opera and symphonic music, could not achieve a satisfactory level of acoustics for either. The 'Review of Program' proposed by the new team of architects was accepted by the government in 1967, and work began on Stage III. Work progressed very slowly while final plans were made: it was not until mid-1969 that the pace of work picked up.

The decision to devote the main hall to concerts meant that around 2700 seats would fit into the area, and that the acoustics could be fine-tuned to the requirements of orchestral music. To the smaller hall, changes were made to fit in with the conception of an intimate opera. Under the Concert Hall, the area that was originally designed to house stage machinery and the scenery dock was converted into the Recording Hall and the Music Room.

The Review of Program, at this fairly late date, meant more cost increases. Enormous amounts had already been spent on staging equipment for the main hall, and most of this had to be scrapped. Although the major users were happier with the new plans, controversy once again caused headlines, with critics of the new plan claiming that the smaller opera hall would not be suitable for many operas and ballets. This controversy, to some extent, still rages today.

> 'I feel the Concert Hall is one of the greatest, if not the greatest, in the world. The acoustic is second to none.'
>
> Dame Joan Sutherland

Acoustical Design

As in any theatre, concert hall or opera house, acoustics were a primary concern, and caused not only difficulties in design, but, as we have seen, major changes to the entire plan. A specialist acoustics designer, Dr Vilhelm Jordan and his son, Niels, worked on the project along with a Professor Cremer, who left the project when the new plan was put in place.

The Australian Broadcasting Commission required a reverberation time of two seconds, but the volume of space within the Concert Hall was limited, and only just sufficient. Vertical side walls are a valuable acoustic feature, but the Opera House had curved walls. The hall was oblong in shape, giving the designers difficulties in ensuring a full sound throughout the hall. The final design incorporated a high ceiling, and a sort of pleated wall design which gave many horizontal surfaces. Prefabricated plywood — in a great variety of sizes — is used in the sculptured ceiling's 1750 panels. Central place is taken by a crown piece of white birch plywood 12.20 metres (40 feet) in diameter, and 24.40 metres (80 feet) above the floor.

Adjustable acoustic rings are suspended directly above the orchestra, providing a 'bounce-back' sound system so that the orchestra can hear themselves.

In spite of the plan to devote the Concert Hall to orchestral music, it has in fact been used for opera, dance, rock concerts and variety shows. The acoustics in this hall have been acclaimed by many critics. Joan Sutherland, the Australian diva, said of them, 'I feel the Concert Hall is one of the greatest, if not the greatest, in the world. The acoustic is second to none'. The *Sydney Morning Herald*'s music critic, Roger Covell, called the acoustics 'revealing to internal disagreements of intonation among the upper strings', but declared that this would just demand a higher standard of performance.

In the Opera Theatre, the seating numbers had been increased by adding back and side balconies, which created further acoustical difficulties. The acoustical designers pushed the ceiling upwards as much as possible and designed hard reflecting surfaces on both sides of the proscenium. The reverberation time in this

hall is 1.4 seconds. There were criticisms of the size of the orchestral pit, which was enlarged in 1994 by extending it back under the stage so it could accommodate 80 musicians, up from 56. It also tends to trap the sound, making it very loud and uncomfortable for the musicians. These criticisms are still around today. Generally, though,

The Concert Hall under construction. (Photo: Max Dupain, courtesy of Max Dupain and Associates Pty Ltd)

At high tide, the Opera House looks very much like a spectacular raft about to drift away to sea. (Photo: Anne Fraser)

The Glass Walls

In 1972 the engineering firm of Ove Arup and Partners was given the annual engineering excellence award of the Association of Consulting Engineers in Australia. Although the firm had been integral to the success of the entire building of the Opera House, the specific work it had done to achieve this distinction was the design and the planning of the great glass walls that enclose the mouths of the huge shells. Like almost every other feature of this building, they were not simple to design or to make. Utzon envisioned the walls as glass curtains, framed by bronze-clad plywood mullions in a complicated series of stepped planes. Before Utzon's resignation, the issue of using plywood seemed to be a hotly contested question, with the government claiming that a consultant from Ove Arup had said that the plywood would not be strong enough: it appears that this advice was later rescinded but the dispute had continued.

Utzon had aimed for an effect of draped glass, but when the panel attempted to carry out his plan, they encountered problems. Abandoning the original plan they, with the help of the engineers, arrived at another plan using steel mullions and two layers of glass.

most operas, except perhaps Wagnarian operas, have been staged successfully, and the acoustics are regarded as good.

The position of the building, almost entirely surrounded by water, meant that there were few external noise problems, except one — the tooting of passenger liners. A number of features helped to exclude these loud sirens: a layer of laminated glazing in the glass areas; an interior, sprayed concrete layer between the foyers and the halls; and the plaster-ply construction of the inner cladding of the halls.

The glass was laminated, and consisted of two sheets — one plain, the other topaz — bonded by a middle layer of transparent synthetic rubber. Enormous amounts were needed — over 6223 square metres (67,000 square feet) in all. The glass, in 2000 pieces, was made in France and shipped to Australia, and with only one or two breakages. The glass-maker, Boussois Souchon Neuvesel based in Boussois in France, was chosen because it was one of the few glass works still producing glass by a pot-casting process, which enabled it to make small quantities in a special colour.

After the structural system had been designed and the materials selected, the problem of assembling it all remained. Special saws were needed to cut the glass; computers were needed to accurately marry the 700 different shapes, and every connection, bolt-hole and piece of glass had to be carefully planned. The system was so complex that, as R. Kelman, an associate partner of Ove Arup and Partners, said, 'nothing could be finalised until everything was'. Everything was interconnected, so even a small change meant reprogramming the whole. In surmounting these complications, the designers and engineers once again broke new ground.

Top: The north-facing glass walls. (Photo: Anne Fraser)

Left: The wonderful shapes of the northern glass walls from the inside. (Courtesy of M. R. Hornibrook Pty Ltd)

Cladding and Upholstery

For the exterior and many interior walls, stairs and floors, a pink aggregate granite facing, quarried at Tarana (in the Blue Mountains west of Sydney), was used. The cladding was not what Utzon had envisaged for the building — he had thoroughly researched the material and had had over 30 samples presented to him before approving one. But procedures were to change after he left the job. David Moore, the well-known photographer, recalls visiting the site when the cladding was being chosen, some years after Utzon's departure. The minister, Davis Hughes, was on the site, and the architects were allowing him to choose the colour of the cladding from about four or five samples. Hughes asked David Moore which one he would chose, but Moore declined to express an opinion, feeling that it was not up to him — or Davis Hughes — to make such an important decision.

Two woods are used throughout the building: brushbox and white birch plywood, both cut in New South Wales. The carpets were made of Australian wool, as was the upholstery for the audience seating. Chairs were designed in continental style and manufactured in white birch plywood, and upholstered in vivid colours: magenta in the Concert Hall, red in the Opera Theatre and a striking vermilion in the Drama Theatre.

Art in the House

Several important artworks grace the Opera House interiors. The most famous is a work in five panels by John Olsen entitled *Five Bells*. Inspired by a Kenneth Slessor poem of the same name, it is positioned in the northern foyer of the Concert Hall. Two other major works are tapestries by the Australian artist John Coburn. In 1969 Coburn was commissioned to create the curtains for the Opera and Drama Theatre. The designs he created were woven by the Aubusson-maker, Pinton Freres, in France, using full-sized enlargements from colour paintings by Coburn. The *Curtain of the Sun*, in the Opera Theatre, features warm tones while its counterpoint, the *Curtain of the Moon*, is used in the Drama Theatre and is woven in the cooler tones of blue and green with areas of yellow, rust and brown.

Other artworks held in the Opera House include *The Bennelong Series* by

Donald Friend, *The Little Shark* by Sidney Nolan, *Ballerina Sketch* by Brett Whiteley, *Possum Dreaming* by Michael Tjakamurra, and *Girl Listening to Music* by Charles Blackman.

The Organ

The Grand Organ in the Concert Hall was designed and built by Australian Ronald Sharp with assistance in the final stages from the Austrian firm of Gregor Hradetzky. It is the largest mechanical-action organ in the world. There is an interesting story behind this organ. Ronald Sharp began work on his plans for it as soon as it was announced that a grand organ for the Concert Hall would be commissioned. Although he had no official contract, he worked on his plans for a full two years — at his own expense — before he was awarded the job by a committee set up to find an organ builder. However, the construction of the organ echoed the problems that had beset the Opera House itself: criticism of the time it took (five years and eight months) and of its rising cost ($1.2 million rather than the $400,000 originally forecast). Perhaps because Ronald Sharp was self-taught,

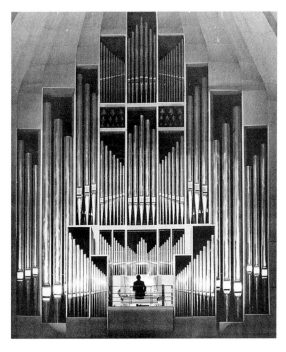

The Grand Organ in the Concert Hall took over five and half years to build.

and Australian rather than European, statements were frequently made in the media lambasting his 'incompetence'. But Ronald Sharp was a perfectionist, and, in a booklet celebrating the organ's completion, he was quoted as saying that he had 'wanted to prove that organs could be made in Australia which were as good or better than those made in other countries'.

Just as with the Opera House itself, the outcries about the organ's cost and the delays melted away once it was finished. In June 1979, when music critics heard the

Two large curtain tapestries woven by Aubusson in France to the designs of John Coburn cover the prosceniums in the Opera Theatre and the Drama Theatre. Shown here is the Curtain of the Moon, *which hangs in the Drama Theatre. (Photo: Courtesy of Ove Arup and Partners)*

only 109 of them are actually visible to the public. With its gleaming pipes of different heights and widths, the organ provides an impressive focal point to the Concert Hall. At its highest point, it towers 24 metres above the stage.

The Car Park

The car park, spiralling downwards beneath the Opera House complex was started in 1990 and completed in 1993. The problem of parking was a constant refrain during the construction phase, but the plans never included the cost of a car park. It was built, financed and is operated by Enacon Parking Pty Ltd under a 50-year lease, after which it will revert to the government. The car park has space for 1100 cars and was the first double helix-shaped underground car park of its type in the world.

'There Stands Our Opera House!'

organ at its very first recital, they gave it high praise. In a tribute to his achievement, a column in the *Sydney Morning Herald* said: 'Ronald Sharp had a dream of an organ for the Opera House that would sing with a thousand soft and stormy voices. After 10 years' work, he has realised that dream ... People are often suspicious of dreamers ... If our dreamer takes too long to deliver the goods, or costs us too much money, we become harshly critical. We drove Jørn Utzon from the Opera House. We came perilously close to doing the same thing to Ronald Sharp.'

Over 10,000 pipes were used, although

When the plan for an Opera House was first discussed at the public meeting called by Premier Cahill in 1954, Lindley Evans, of the Musical Society of New South Wales, enthused, 'What a wonderful thing it would be for all the thousands of people who come to Sydney Harbour to see a magnificent building on that point and to be told with pride by Sydney people 'There stands our Opera House!' The vision of a great performing centre for Sydney, housed in an important and striking building, was merely a dream then — a dream that was only just beginning to emerge. Now, nearly half a century since those hopeful words were spoken, the dream is reality.

The Opera House is a vibrant arts centre, and the rift with its creator now healed in the cause of refitting it for the twenty-first century. The interiors may be improved and updated, techniques of repair modernised, and access enhanced, but the building itself cannot be improved upon. Like all truly great buildings, it has a timeless appeal. The Opera House is as breathtaking today as it was on its opening day.

In the years between 1958 and 1973, Bennelong Point was transformed from the bus station (above), to the magnificent completed Opera House (left). (Photos courtesy of Ove Arup and Partners)

'Today Utzon showed us over the Opera House … It has made me feel glad I am alive in Australia today. At last we are going to have something worth having.'

Patrick White, in a 1963 letter to Desmond Digby, in Patrick White, Letters, *edited by David Marr.*

The Performing Arts: An Overview

To understand how the Sydney Opera House came to be built and its vital role in the nation's artistic life, one must understand a little of the history of the performing arts in Australia.

In 1788, the First Fleet sailed into Sydney Cove with 1030 people, including 736 convicts. Not a very auspicious beginning for the flowering of a rich artistic culture. And yet within 18 months, on 4 June 1789, the first play was performed in a makeshift hut. A cast of convicts, directed by Lieutenant Ralph Clark, performed the comedy *The Recruiting Officer* by George Farquhar to celebrate the birthday of King George III. By 1832, Sydney had its first purpose-built theatre, the Theatre Royal.

Above: The Royal Victoria Theatre opened in March 1838, and was, along with the Theatre Royal, one of the first of many theatres to be built in colonial Sydney.

The first 'operatic' performance seems to have been *The Poor Soldier* by William Shield performed in 1796. Unfortunately, though, nothing is known about this first operatic performance in Australia.

The records for ballet performances in the nineteenth century are very scant too but we do have a record of a ballet entitled *La Fille Mal Gardée* being performed in 1855 by a visiting French dancer, Aurelia Dimier.

It would be wrong, however, to imagine that these performances resembled anything like the operas and ballets we see today in the Sydney Opera House. Mostly, what was called an opera was an evening's entertainment of songs, stiffly performed, without a set, orchestra or costumes; and the ballet was a segment of the 'opera', usually consisting of a dance such as a polka or a Highland fling or even acrobats on stilts. It appears that the 'ballet' was really only an excuse for men to look at women's legs, and in a society that had a shortage of women, it is not surprising the ballet was the main attraction of the evening. After the 'opera' and 'ballet', the evening's entertainment was capped off with a drama or farce. Performers were expected to take part in all three entertainments — dancing, singing and acting.

By the 1850s, people were flocking to Australia to make their fortunes on the newly discovered gold fields. With this dramatic increase in population came an upsurge in the need for entertainment. Many theatrical companies were established and overseas artists came to tour Australia. One of the more notorious was Lola Montez, who took her provocative Spider Dance to Ballarat, where, instead of being showered with flowers, she was thrown gold nuggets. When she did her

show in Sydney, Lola's popularity was so great that the management decided to abandon the usual custom of charging women half price if accompanied by a man.

The most important impresario to arrive in Australia was James Cassius Williamson, an American actor, whose company, J.C. Williamson, was to have a great influence on the development of professional drama, opera and ballet in Australia.

In 1911, Williamson backed a tour of the first complete opera company of 200, including principals, chorus and full orchestra and starring Nellie Melba. They opened on 2 September with *La Traviata* and did fabulous business, creating a great demand for opera. Opera was so popular that in Melbourne in 1924 Melba had a 12-week season that included 16 operas. During the season, 211,200 tickets were sold to a population of only 885,700.

In 1893, J.C. Williamson staged the first classical ballet, *Turquiosette or A Study in Blue*, along with three operas, for a six-week season, commencing in Melbourne, then touring to Sydney, Adelaide and Ballarat. The

company boasted 100 dancers, including Catherine Bartho from Moscow and Enrichetta d'Argo from Naples.

But it wasn't until 1913 that Australians were to see their first proper ballet. Adeline Genée came to Australia with a number of dancers from the Imperial Russian Ballet and performed *Coppelia* and some of Fokine's works, including *The Dying Swan*.

In 1926 and 1929, Anna Pavlova toured Australia. Although she was in decline and her company was not particularly good, her appearance in Australia boosted the development of ballet and a number of ballet schools were started.

One of her dancers from the 1929 tour was Edouard Borovansky, who returned to Australia in 1938 with the de Basil's company and stayed to start the Borovansky Ballet, which eventually became the Australian Ballet in 1962. Peggy van Praagh was brought from England to be the founding artistic director. It was her efforts in nurturing a new generation of Australian artists, including choreographers like Graeme Murphy, who became artistic director of the Sydney Dance Company, and Meryl Tankard, who became artistic director of the Australian Dance Company in South Australia.

Robert Helpmann was appointed co-artistic director of the Australian Ballet and in 1964 put on the first all-Australian work, *The Display*, complete with beer drinking and bush picnic.

Purely orchestral performances were very rare in the early days. Mostly, orchestras were used for operas and ballets. Occasionally, J.C. Williamson brought out lavish orchestras for an extravaganza but otherwise orchestral music, if it ever was performed, was very crude.

It wasn't until the 1930s, when the Australian Broadcasting Commission (ABC) was set up, that a permanent government-subsidised orchestra was founded. Known as the ABC (Sydney) Symphony Orchestra, it was a radio studio orchestra intended to play everything from light music to cut-down symphonies.

Before the ABC was set up there had been one professional orchestra, the Sydney Symphony Orchestra, that played between 1908 and 1914. There had also been the New South Wales State Orchestra, which was a permanent group. Mostly, in the 1920s, musical life revolved around the theatre, cinema and the student orchestras from the State's Conservatorium music school.

The orchestras at this time were enthusiastic but lacked proper training and often had to make do with inferior instruments. In 1934, guest conductor Sir Hamilton Harty, who conducted the first major concert at the Sydney Town Hall, complained that the double basses were 'wretchedly bad' and that at times the trombones were 'coarse and uncertain in pitch'.

The Sydney Symphony Orchestra came of age under the acclaimed English-born conductor Eugene Goossens, who was the

Above: Margot Fonteyn taking her curtain call at the conclusion of Raymondo *with the Australian Ballet company in 1971.*

Left: Edouard Borovansky in L'Amour Ridicule. *(Courtesy of the Australian Ballet)*

The program of the 1948 Old Vic Theatre tour which starred Laurence Olivier and Vivien Leigh.

orchestra's principal conductor from 1946 to 1955. For the first time, Sydney audiences heard new music, including home-grown Australian music. Just after Goossens arrived, he conducted John Antill's *Corroboree* at the Town Hall and received an eight-minute standing ovation. Musically, things were on the move. It was the result of Goossens' efforts to find the orchestra a permanent home that the Sydney Opera House was built.

Musica Viva, the well-known Opera House company for chamber music, was founded in late 1945 by Richard Goldner. By 1955 the society was importing overseas groups and has grown to be one of the world's biggest entrepreneurial organizations of its type.

In 1954, the performing arts, for the first time in Australia, received substantial government financial support following the setting up of the Australian Elizabethan Theatre Trust. In 1956 the Trust, for all intents and purposes, established the Australian Opera with its 1956 Mozart bicentennial season, although the Australian Opera was not formally constituted until 1970. In 1960, in association with J.C. Williamson, the Trust supported the fledgling Australian Ballet. In drama, the Trust tended to support imported

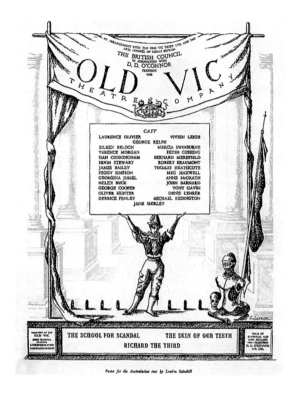

Poster for the Australasian tour by Loudon Spindhill

productions, rather than setting up a national theatre company.

Drama is not as expensive to stage as opera or ballet. Consequently, between the wars Sydney had a large number of amateur companies. Actors worked in radio by day and performed in amateur theatre at night. Large commercial shows toured Australia in the 1940s and 1950s — musicals like *South Pacific* and *Annie Get Your Gun*. An Old Vic tour with Laurence

Olivier and Vivien Leigh in 1948 made an enormous impact on the theatre scene in Australia, but it wasn't until 1968 that an initiative to set up a flagship theatre company in each state was undertaken. The competition to become the state theatre company for NSW was battled out between the Independent, the Ensemble and the Old Tote. The Old Tote won. In 1973 the Old Tote Company opened its first Opera House season with Bertolt Brecht's *Threepenny Opera*, though its first production for the opening of the Drama Theatre had been Shakespeare's *Richard II*.

In retrospect, the Sydney Opera House couldn't have opened at a better time. In 1973 the arts in Australia were starting to feel a fresh, invigorating breeze blowing from Canberra. After 23 years of being out in the cold, the Australian Labor Party under Gough Whitlam had taken office. One of the new government's platforms was to give support and assistance to the arts. Suddenly the arts were getting a bit of the limelight. There was a feeling of opening up and the possibility that anything could be tried. This excitement was very much evident in the programming of the first few years of the Sydney Opera House. The diversity was staggering. It

Eugene Goossens — one of the prime movers in getting an opera house for Sydney, and the principal conductor of the Sydney Symphony Orchestra from 1946 to 1955. (Photo courtesy of ABC Document Archives)

was a venue for new experimental works that otherwise would have been unlikely to see the light of day. Unfortunately, more recently, as a result of financial constraints, there has been less of the enthusiastic experimentation of those early days.

'For what greater
inspiration could an
architect wish than to
design a building to house
the fruits of human
culture?'

*Jørn Utzon, quoted in the
Australian, 19 October 1973*

The Busiest Performance Centre in the World

The Sydney Opera House was officially opened on 20 October 1973. But before this there were in fact many preliminary performances.

Probably the first person to 'perform' at the Opera House was Paul Robeson, when he sang in 1960 to the construction workers. However the first official performances were the many test performances given in each of the performing spaces before the Opera House was open to the public.

It was not until September 1973 that the public, who had lived with the building's vicissitudes for so long, was at last going to see if it was going 'to perform' to expectations. Not everyone expected that it would. The first performance open to the public was the Australian Opera's production of Prokofiev's *War and Peace*, on 28 September 1973 in the Opera Theatre. It was produced by the American

Sam Wanamaker with fabulous sets by Tom Lingwood. It had a huge cast, giving Sydney its first taste of how spectacular opera was going to be in the Opera House. Despite the rumours that the Opera Theatre was inadequate for large productions and impossible to work in, Wanamaker did manage to produce a stunning production.

Roger Covell of the *Sydney Morning Herald*, remarked in his review that the sound from the orchestra pit had much improved since the test performances, the only problem being the thinness in the strings — the unavoidable result of the shortage of violins in the over-crowded pit.

The following day, the Concert Hall offered up its first public performance which consisted entirely of Wagner performed by the Sydney Symphony Orchestra, conducted by Charles Mackerras with soloist soprano Birgit Nilsson.

In the Drama Theatre, two days later on 1 October, the Old Tote Theatre Company (which was to become the Sydney Theatre Company in 1978), performed Shakespeare's *Richard II*, directed by Robin Lovejoy. Harry Kippax, the drama critic for the *Australian*, was most unflattering about the Drama Theatre. He described it as the 'bargain basement of the Opera House' and said the foyer was sombre and antiseptic, with low ceilings. This fortunately has changed since Kippax's day: the foyer today has been extended to join the Playhouse foyer, giving a spacious feeling.

Hot on its heals, Musica Viva presented the Carl Pini Quartet in the Music Room on 2 October. Then, within days, on 5 October, a program of contemporary trombone music, performed by Stuart Dempster, was presented in the Recording Hall.

The Exhibition Hall opened before them all with *All the World's a Stage* on

25 September and, finally, in the Reception Hall an exhibition of paintings on 28 October was presented by artist Robert Emerson Curtis.

The Official Opening

Queen Elizabeth II and the Duke of Edinburgh arrived for the ceremonies on Saturday 20 October. The day dawned bright and sunny, though rather windy and the harbour was filled with craft of all sorts participating in a sort of marine parade.

There were over 15,000 official guests but the crowd outside, in the area around the Opera House and in the Botanic Gardens, swelled to around one million people. The ceremony itself involved the unveiling of a plaque by the Queen. Amongst all of the dignitaries, one absence was noted and commented on by the press: Jørn Utzon had not accepted the government's invitation to attend the opening of the building. It would be many years before this rift was healed.

The opening was followed in the evening by a display of fireworks and a concert featuring Beethoven's Symphony No.9 in D minor and an Australian piece, *Jubugalee*, by John Antill.

Time *magazine's cover in October 1973 celebrated the long-awaited opening. (Reproduced courtesy of Time Magazine; photo David Moore)*

Something for Everyone

In the beginning, the Sydney Opera House was host to all sorts of shows, from formal symphonies and chamber music to pop concerts, Sunday night variety shows and, on one occasion, even a boxing match. On that particular evening the audience erupted at the end of the match and had their own massive punch-up in the Concert Hall. The Opera House staff looked on aghast at the image of the Concert Hall being trashed. Security stepped in and managed to stop the fighting before too much damage was done.

Another regular event in the early days was mass baptisms which were held in an enormous pool set up in the centre of the Concert Hall. Hundreds of crying babies and children were dunked in the pool, water slopping everywhere. It was not a popular event with Opera House staff who dreaded an evening mopping up water. Perhaps rather more poignant is the story of the young guitarist who believed he only needed a public solo performance for his career to be made. He hired the Concert Hall but, apart from the three front of house staff, only two other people sat in the audience! Since these early days the hiring policy has tightened up a great deal.

Even so, the Opera House still plays host to some wonderful acts such as the Sydney Festival 2000's popular Cardoso Flea Circus, in which a Colombian artist put her fleas through their paces, high-diving, walking the tight-rope and being shot out of a thimble-size cannon.

The first Sunday Variety concert was on 30 September 1973 and featured Rolf Harris at seat prices of $5 to $15. He was followed by Petula Clark, Johnny Farnham, Carol Burnett, Dave Allen, Helen Reddy and many others. The Concert Hall has always been a popular venue, especially before the opening of the Sydney Entertainment Centre in 1983 and, more recently, of Angel Place. Such well-known artists as Cilla Black, Charles Aznavour, Ella Fitzgerald, Count Basie, Donovan, Tiny Tim, Joni Mitchell, Kerrie Biddel and Tony Bennett have all made an appearance in the Concert Hall. Jazz duet Cleo Lane and Johnny Dankworth appeared a couple of times in the 1980s. South African singer Miriam Makeba appeared in 1995, kd lang in 1996, and comedian Billy Connolly has been a long-time favourite.

Apart from a lot of variety, the Opera House provided a venue for more experimental pieces that would otherwise have been restricted to obscure venues and smaller audiences. This was especially true of the old Recording Hall, affectionately known as the R and R (recording and rehearsal studio). Unlike the bigger halls, the atmosphere here was less formal. The audiences were not huge but they came with an air of enthusiasm for something different.

Cabaret, always popular, was at its best in the R and R. Robyn Archer, who wrote and directed the cabaret show, *The Conquest of Carmen Miranda*, starring Noni

Hazlehurst, captured all the atmosphere of a decadent European cabaret — people sitting around drinking in an atmosphere thick with cigarette smoke.

Today the rough and ready R and R is no longer — in its place is the smarter Studio. The Studio is very adaptable and is used for many types of events including media releases. It was here that the Australian Olympic Games uniforms were first revealed to the world.

Free outdoor entertainment around the broadwalks was — and still is, although not

Nancye Hayes as Roxie Hart in the 1981 production of Chicago *staged in the Drama Theatre. She is sitting in Terence Donovan's lap who is playing Billy Flynn. (Photo: Brett Hilder)*

in such profusion — available as part of the 'Sundays around the House' program. In the early days the Trust also provided free Sunday concerts in the Recording Hall but unfortunately, with increased costs and the need to turn a dollar, these free regular indoor events have ceased. The outdoor entertainment is very varied and can include anything from brass and jazz bands, dance and song, to strolling minstrels, street theatre and clowns. One of the big annual attractions was the Folkloric festival that was held on the forecourt. This is now known as the Festival of Cultures.

One of the policies of the Sydney Opera House Trust has been to encourage the participation of children and young people in the arts. In 1979 it introduced its Bennelong program — a series of low-cost daytime programs designed to introduce people of all ages to opera, ballet, drama, chamber music, symphony concerts, jazz and so on. By 1983, apart from 70 performances being staged, workshops on choreography, set-making, costume design and master classes in jazz were being offered.

Innovative music programs for the very young, the Babies Proms, which have been immensely popular over the years, were introduced and followed later by the Primary Proms.

A number of the regular companies have been participating over the years, devising programs especially for children and high school students. For example, the Sydney Dance Company has a program called Insights in Dance that demonstrates the diverse creative and practical aspects of staging dance. Even guest companies have participated in bringing the performing arts to the young. The Perth Theatre Company in 1997 did a production of *Lockie Leonard Human Torpedo,* adapted from the extremely popular novel by Tim Winton.

The Marionette Theatre of Australia in the early days was a regular company of the Opera House, performing puppet shows for

Kiri Te Kanawa performing at the Concert Hall. (Photo: Don McMurdo)

the young and old alike. *General MacArthur in Australia* was especially devised for adult audiences and performed in the Drama Theatre in the evenings. The puppets were designed by the well-known cartoonist Patrick Cook.

The first organ concert took place on 7 June 1979, but it took a couple of years for the instrument to play at its best. By 1982 it was in full swing with English organist, Peter Hurford, together with guitarist John Williams appearing in a sell-out Bach concert.

A Focus for the Arts

One of the most important effects of the Opera House on the arts in Australia arose from the attention it attracted. The world had become aware of the Opera House through following the trials and tribulations of its construction. Once it was opened, international attention focussed on what was going on beneath its sails.

Not only were travellers making a night at the Opera House a priority of their visit to the city, but international artists were pencilling the Sydney Opera House into their engagement dairies. Despite some criticisms of the inside, especially of the Opera Theatre, the acoustics of the Concert Hall were wonderful and lured many international artists.

Many international artists have performed at the Opera House, including Kiri Te Kanawa, the renowned New Zealand soprano, who wrote that she 'always loved performing in the Sydney Opera House, despite all its inadequacies, as the productions often have an Australian flair and freshness, an uninhibited Australian magic'. Another early visitor to the Opera House was Leonard Bernstein and the New York Philharmonic Orchestra who gave two performances to absolutely packed houses.

Vladimir Ashkenazy is no stranger to the Opera House and has appeared many times. Most recently, in January 2000, leading the Philharmonia Orchestra he conducted Mahler's *Ninth*. Peter McCullum wrote: '[it] was one of the finest things I have heard in the Opera House Concert Hall.' His charity recital in 1982, when the audience was treated to an evening of his exquisite playing of Chopin to raise money for micro-surgery, will be long remembered with affection and feeling by Sydney audiences.

International troupes frequently visit the Opera House, giving Sydneysiders the opportunity to see what is going on in other parts of the world. The China Beijing Opera troupe, en route to the Melbourne

Festival, delighted audiences in 1995 with their costumes, acrobatics, strange singing dialogue and high-pitched songs. A Danish company, Hotel Pro Forma, gave a performance in 1997 that defied categorisation —an extraordinary and original piece of theatre that could best be described as visual opera, musical theatre in an abstract painting. The Gypsies came in 1997 and performed their passionate earthy music with jubilance and were cheered off the stage.

The Opera House has been the home of the Sydney Dance Company and the venue for many exciting new Australian ballets. The Australian Ballet, though based in Melbourne, Victoria, usually appears at the Sydney Opera House for its Sydney season.

The Drama Theatre and the Playhouse have hosted some of Australia's most memorable and important stage productions and have seen actors like Mel Gibson, Judy Davis, Geoffrey Rush, Leo McKern, Hugo Weaving and Richard Roxburgh walk its boards.

The Opera House has seen the birth of two regular companies: the Australian Chamber Orchestra, founded in 1975, which has been very successful and built its reputation in the Concert Hall; and the

Leo McKern, of Rumpole fame, in the Sydney Theatre Company's 1999 production of She Stoops to Conquer. *(Photo: Branco Gaica)*

Sydney Theatre Company, formed in 1978, which grew out of the Old Tote Theatre Company. The Drama Theatre remained the Sydney Theatre Company's principal home until 1984 when it moved to its present premises at the Wharf Theatre. Today it does some five productions a year at the Opera House and shares the venue with touring companies and the Sydney Dance Company. Recently, the Bell Shakespeare Company has been performing

Dame Joan Sutherland's farewell performance in 1991 on the final night of Les Huguenots. (Photo: Don McMurdo)

regularly at the Opera House, usually in the Playhouse.

In 1997 the Australian Opera joined forces with the Victoria State Opera to become Opera Australia. Though based in Sydney, it divides its season between Sydney and Melbourne. Opera Australia gives between 240 and 250 performances of more than 20 operas a year. In fact, it is the third busiest opera company in the world.

One of the most cherished singers of Australian opera is the now-retired Dame Joan Sutherland. Dame Joan's debut at the

Opera House was made in a Concert Hall recital on 6 July 1974, with her husband, Richard Bonynge, accompanying her on the piano. Her first appearance with the Australian Opera was seven days later in *The Tales of Hoffmann*. She was an enormous success and 'brought the audience to the highest pitch of excitement'.

Sutherland made many appearances on the opera stage at the Opera House until her final farewell performance in 1991 in *Les Huguenots,* where she played Marguerite de Valois with Richard Bonynge conducting. Always tremendously popular with audiences and everyone backstage, she very much made the Sydney Opera House her own. She played many roles, from the flighty Rosalinde in Johann Strauss' *Die Fledermaus* to her renowned performance as tragic Lucia in Donizetti's *Lucia di Lammermoor*. When Sutherland returned to play Lucia in 1986 she was 59 and yet she sounded like a 25-year-old soprano, only better. Her performance was magnificent and led critic John Cargher to write that Sutherland's 'singing that night was close to the best in her career'.

Many of the world's great singers were now attracted to the idea of appearing at the Opera House. Luciano Pavarotti, who had been here in 1965, appearing with Joan Sutherland, returned in 1983 to appear in a Gala performance with Joan Sutherland and the Elizabethan Symphony Orchestra conducted by Richard Bonynge. People queued all night to get tickets. Seats were from $20 to $150 and even then it was immediately over-subscribed. More than 6 million people watched the televised performance.

Other singers came. Rita Hunter even settled in Sydney. Jessye Norman first appeared in the Concert Hall in a recital in 1976 with the Sydney Symphony Orchestra and then returned in 1981 to packed houses. Dame Kiri Te Kanawa made her debut in Australia at the Opera House in *La Boheme* in 1976. More recently, in 1999 the Welsh baritone Bryn Terfel performed with the Sydney Symphony Orchestra under Edo de Waart, and also with Opera Australia in *Falstaff*. The world-renowned Philip Glass performed his *Koyaanisqatsi* and was one of the first performers to appear in the Concert Hall in 2000. Though first performed in 1983, it still managed to hypnotise the audience with its extraordinary mix of film and music and unique way of seeing the patterns of life.

Dame Joan Sutherland in her most famous role, Lucia, in the 1980 production of Lucia Di Lammermoor. *(Photo: Don McMurdo)*

Opera highlights

There have been many opera highlights at the Opera House. One of the earliest was an outstanding production of Janácek's *Jenöfa* in 1974. Directed by John Copley with designs by Alan Lees, it featured the young South African mezzo soprano, Elizabeth Connell, who gave an outstanding performance. She was soon to become an international star.

In 1975, the Australian Opera performed Verdi's *Aida* in the Concert Hall with Carlo Felice Cillario conducting. *Aida* was too large for the Opera Theatre, but staging it in the Concert Hall posed enormous problems. The Concert Hall after all was designed for orchestral concerts, so it didn't have an orchestra pit. Or wings. Or facilities to fly scenery. Tom Lingwood overcame these problems by cleverly incorporating the majestic ceiling with its rolling curves into the actual set so that the opera became a part of the Concert Hall. It was an enormous success. A more recent production of *Aida* in 1995 was conducted by Australian-born Simone Young. Young made her debut at the Sydney Opera House in 1985 when she was only 24 years old, and since has become a leading international conductor. She returns in 2001 to become Opera Australia's music director, taking over from retiring artistic director Moffat Oxenbould.

Another sell-out production was *La Traviata* in 1978, directed by John Copley and starring the young New Zealand soprano Kiri Te Kanawa singing Violetta. It was so popular that an extra Sunday performance had to be put on to cater for the New Zealanders arriving in plane-loads from New Zealand to see their own famous soprano.

La Traviata was the opera chosen for the first Opera in the Park in 1982. Joan Sutherland sang the title role. These free performances were to prove extremely popular and brought opera to thousands of people, many of whom would never have gone to see opera in a theatre.

Mussorgsky's *Boris Godunov*, starring Donald Shanks and produced by Elijah Moshinsky, was the highlight for 1980. The headline to Maria Prerauer's review punned, 'It's not just Godunov — it's superb!' The other major production of the year was

Janácek's *Katya Kabanova*, starring Marilyn Richardson.

Handel's *Alcina* in 1981 was an unlikely hit. Directed by Sir Robert Helpmann, this opera, usually only of interest to the aficionado, turned into a box-office sensation through Helpmann's imaginative and dramatic staging.

The Australian Opera had a big year in 1983. Jennifer McGregor sang Lucia in *Lucia di Lammermoor* to enormous acclaim, with critics writing a 'star is born'. The same year saw Opera in the Park quadruple its numbers and Sir Robert Helpmann direct a new production of *Roméo et Juliette* by Charles Gounod, which, as usual, brought the opera to life.

Pavarotti also appeared as Rodolfo in 1983 in three performances of Andrew Sinclair's production of *La Boheme*. unfortunately this was not quite the hit that people had hoped it would be, and by all accounts it didn't match the exciting Baz Luhrmann production staged seven years later in 1990 — an extraordinary fresh and emotionally charged production set in the 1950s. Handsome David Hobson played Rodolfo, and beautiful Cheryl Barker played the frail Mimi.

According to one critic, it was so popular that David Hobson practically became a matinee idol. It was only supposed to be a cheap fill-in production, at only $65,000, but instead it proved to be one of the Australian Opera's biggest hits. One of its striking contrasts with earlier productions of *La Boheme*, apart from the magnificent designs by Catherine Martin, was the consummate acting. Opera singers are not always good actors and it was in no small part the acting quality of this production that led critic Peter Cochrane in the *Sydney Morning Herald* to write that *La*

Aida in the Concert Hall, 1975. The designer Tom Lingwood overcame the problems of setting the opera in a hall that had no proscenium arch or wings by incorporating the curves of the ceiling of the Concert Hall into the set. (Photo: Don McMurdo)

Michael Lewis in the 1990 production of Rigoletto which was set in the 1950s. Instead of being a hunchback Rigoletto was a cripple with walking sticks. (Photo: Don McMurdo)

Boheme 'led an opera rebirth'. No-one in the audience could ever forget in the final scene the magnetic power of Hobson's acting — he stood on a ladder and openly wept to an utterly silent stage while the audience sat spellbound.

In the same year, Elijah Moshinsky's production of Verdi's opera *Rigoletto* was also set in the 1950s, with the Count surrounded by Mafia-style henchmen. Rigoletto, instead of being a hunchback, was a cripple with two walking sticks

and Gilda an engaging youngster in bobby socks.

Bizet's *Carmen* has had many performances at the Opera House. In 1987 John Copley did an interesting non-realistic production in a semi-modern setting. In 1995, Lindy Hume broke with the usual sexual wild cat stereotype of Carmen and instead had Suzanne Johnston play Carmen as a woman fighting to remain her own boss.

Another favourite with audiences is *Madam Butterfly*. A number of productions have been mounted at the Opera House, sung by sopranos including Australian Joan Carden, American Leona Mitchell and, more recently, Cheryl Barker in a new and exciting production of Moffat Oxenbould's.

It has become apparent that the most popular operas and ballets are productions of popular works that take a fresh look and are dramatically updated. Another example of a classic that succeeded because of its refreshed treatment was the 1991 *Turandot*, produced by Graeme Murphy of the Sydney Dance Company. Murphy gave the production an agility not seen before. The production returned in 1995 and Fred Blanks of the

Two very popular and successful operas performed over the years at the Sydney Opera House. Top left: The simple but very effective set of the renowned 1990 production of La Boheme. Top: David Hobson as Rodolfo and Cheryl Barker as Mimi in the same successful 1990 production of La Boheme. Left: Gillian Sullivan in the new 1994 production of La Traviata. (Photos: Don McMurdo)

Sydney Morning Herald described Murphy's staging as exerting 'a thrilling fascination', and said that Leona Mitchell's voice 'reigned with a commanding and sustained magnificence'.

A noticeable trend has been for more operas to be staged by theatre and screen directors, giving them a new dramatic interpretation that was often lacking in earlier more conventional productions. Baz Luhrmann, for example, was a film director who had made a big impact with his film *Strictly Ballroom*. After his great success with *La Boheme*, he returned to the Opera House in 1993 to produce the opera *A Midsummers Night's Dream*. Other well-known drama directors who occasionally switch to opera include Neil Armfield, who did, amongst others, a wonderful production of *Tristan and Isolde* in 1990 with the late Stuart Challender conducting; and Barry Kosky, who occasionally has caused great controversy with his often outlandish productions of operas and plays. Many of his productions concentrate on highlighting the archetypal rather than the individual character. In 1999 Kosky directed Alban Berg's *Wozzeck*, the latest addition to Opera Australia's repertoire.

Australian Operas

The very first opera performed at the Opera House was actually an Australian opera by Larry Sitsky. Another Australian opera, *Rites of Passage* by Peter Sculthorpe, was scheduled for the actual opening of the Opera House but it wasn't completed in time and wasn't performed until 1974. Sculthorpe's *Rites* was more of a mixture of ballet and a chorus without soloists. In the same year, Larry Sitsky's one-act opera *Lenz* was also performed as a double bill with another Australian one-act opera, *The Affair*, by Felix Werder.

The first major Australian opera to appear at the Opera House was most certainly *Voss* in 1987. Adapted from Patrick White's novel of the same name, the opera was an extraordinary accomplishment both musically and dramatically. Composed by Richard Meale with libretto by novelist David Malouf, it told the story of Voss's tragic trip to the interior of Australia (based on the travels of the explorer Ludwig Leichhardt) and the strange unconsummated love between Voss and Laura that gives him spiritual strength. The opera was directed by Jim Sharman, well-known for directing musicals (he did

Two important Australian operas performed by the Australian Opera in the Opera Theatre. Above: David Hobson and Clare Gormley in The Eighth Wonder, *an interesting opera about the building of the Opera House. (Photo: Don McMurdo)*
Right: Geoffrey Chard (top left) as Voss in the opera of the same name based on the novel by Patrick White. Marilyn Richardson as Laura (in white), Greg Tomlinson (top right), Anne Marie Macdonald (bottom left) and Heather Begg (bottom right). (Photo: Don McMurdo)

the original Sydney version of *Hair*) and stage plays, especially plays by Patrick White. Laura was sung by Marilyn Richardson and Voss by Geoffrey Chard. It was not an easy opera, and was criticised for having a difficult plot that was hard to fathom if you didn't know the book.

The Golem was commissioned by the Australian Opera for its 1993 season. It is based on the enduring myth of a creature being created and then getting out of control. The Golem falls in love with its creator, who is a rabbi's daughter, and then ends by going on a killing spree. Composed by Larry Sitsky with libretto by poet Gwen Harwood and directed by Barrie Kosky, it featured Kerry Henderson as the Golem. Most reviewers gave it nothing but praise. Maria Prerauer of the *Australian* wrote: 'This is the most powerful new music-theatre work ever to come from the pen of an Australian composer'.

The third great Australian opera that has been produced at the Opera House in 1995 was *The Eighth Wonder*. An intriguing work, it is about the building of the Sydney Opera House, intertwined with the story of a young conservatorium singer whose ambition is to perform at the new opera house. Jørn Utzon was played by David Hobson (the 'matinee idol' from *La Boheme*). It was directed by Neil Armfield and Brian Thompson designed the sets. Dennis Watkins wrote the libretto and Alan John wrote the music.

There have been other Australian operas: for example in October 1991 *Mer de Glace* by Richard Meale, in collaboration with novelist David Malouf, was staged; Richard Mill's *Summer of the Seventeenth Doll*, based on the stage play by Ray Lawler, was in the 1999 season.

Wagner

Every major opera company aims to have a brilliant *Ring Cycle*; probably the hardest, biggest and most expensive series of operas to stage. But unfortunately the Opera Theatre, with its cramped orchestra pit and lack of stage space, is almost an impossible venue to stage Wagner, so most Wagnerian works are performed in the Concert Hall.

The 1990 *Tristan and Isolde* production — a collaboration between the Sydney Symphony Orchestra and the Australian Opera conducted by Stuart Challender — was a high point in the season. It was directed by stage director Neil Armfield and designed by Brian Thomson. Tragically, Stuart Challender was to die in the following year so the return 1993 production was conducted by Carlo Felice Cillario with Horst Hoffman as Tristan and Marilyn Richardson as Isolde. Roger Covell writes of Richardson's performance as 'unforgettable ... moving and acting with flawless aptness, and constantly surprising us with the amount and quality of the tone she does manage to project'.

Concert versions of Wagner have been successful. Wagner was performed in the first public concert in the Concert Hall, and again in 1977 when *Parsifal* was performed. *Parsifal* lasted for six and a half hours. It was the first occasion, in what was to become a trend for epic works, when the interval was an hour and a half long and designed to coincide with dinner, giving patrons the opportunity to eat at one of the Opera House restaurants or dine outside from their own hampers. The atmosphere was very festive.

Starting in 1995 with *Das Rheingold*, the complete *Ring Cycle* in concert under the baton of Edo de Waart concluded in September 2000 with *Twilight of the Gods* (*Götterdämmerung*) at the end of the 2000 Olympic Arts Festival. The *Sydney Morning*

Marilyn Richardson and Horst Hoffman in Tristan and Isolde, *1993. One of the most successful Wagnerian operas performed by Opera Australia. (Photo: Don McMurdo)*

Herald's headline in 1997 for the *Die Walküre* of the cycle was: 'You just can't keep a good Valkyrie down'. *Siegfried* was the next in the cycle, performed in 1999.

The most successful Wagnerian opera in the Opera Theatre has been *Die Meistersinger von Nürnberg*, performed in 1988 and 1994. The *Sydney Morning Herald* critic wrote: 'This is certainly one of the leading achievements of music theatre in the country and must not be missed by anyone'.

Apart from opera

The Sydney Symphony Orchestra playing in the Concert Hall of the Sydney Opera House. (Courtesy of Sydney Symphony Orchestra)

The original priority of the Sydney Opera House was to give the Sydney Symphony Orchestra a home, opera being a secondary consideration. Utzon's original brief had been to make the Concert Hall a multipurpose venue, but after he left, after much intense lobbying and wrangling, the new architectural panel produced a hall best suited to choral and orchestral concerts. Though some of the members of the SSO found the acoustics a bit clinical, it gave a clarity to the music that their old home, the Sydney Town Hall, hadn't. After the opening concert, Roger Covell commented that the prelude to *Tristan and Isolde* 'resonated ... as if the hall itself were a large cello'.

When the Opera House opened, the Sydney Symphony Orchestra was led by Willem van Otterloo. Sydney has always been a great Mahler city and this was further enhanced by Otterloo, who is probably best remembered for being one of Australia's finest Mahler and Bruckner conductors. His wonderful concert of Mahler's *Fifth* in 1976 was, according to Roger Covell 'one of the major experiences of concert going'.

Sir Charles Mackerras, who had conducted the official opening concert at the Opera House, introduced a very ambitious program during his time as chief conductor from 1982 to 1986. He included works by Webern and Schoenberg, the first performance of Wagner's Symphony in C, Meale's *Very High Kings,* and Janácek's *Glagolitic Mass*. These were not always very popular with audiences. But his 1984 performances of Berlioz's *The Trojans* were significant events in Australia's musical history.

When Stuart Challender took over the Sydney Symphony Orchestra in 1987, he was the orchestra's first Australian resident chief conductor. Some believe that the SSO really became a first-rate reliable orchestra under the guidance of Stuart Challender. Until then the SSO had always tended to be a little like the famous curate's egg: wonderful in parts. This improvement during the Challender years was due to the enormous amount of work Challender put into the orchestra and to a number of internal structural changes. Though the orchestra had had fine chief conductors in the past, because of other commitments, they often did not work as closely with the orchestra as Challender did.

Challender was a champion of Australian composers and in his first season he chose Carl Vine's *Symphony No.2* and Peter Sculthorpe's *Mangrove*. The following years he went on to do Sculthorpe's *Kakadu* which has been played many times since. He was also a conductor of Mahler; Fred Blanks described him as 'Australia's most persuasive Mahlerian'. In June 1990, now quite ill from AIDS, he undertook the enormous task of conducting Mahler's *The Song of the Earth* with soloists Elizabeth Campbell and Robert Tear.

Above: The Toy Symphony gives people a chance to experience what it is like to play in an orchestra. Below: Edo de Waart conducting the Sydney Symphony Orchestra. (Photos: Courtesy of Sydney Symphony Orchestra)

Guests of the Sydney Symphony Orchestra. Top: John Williams. Bottom: Maestro Carlo Rizzi. Top right: The Sydney Symphony Orchestra playing during the Beethoven Festival in 1998. (Photos: Courtesy of Sydney Symphony Orchestra)

In the same month, he conducted Mahler's *Resurrection Symphony*, which is one of his best remembered performances. He died on 13 December 1991.

Edo de Waart became the Orchestra's chief conductor and artistic director in 1992. Under his leadership the orchestra has enjoyed many artistic and critical successes. In 1998 all the Beethoven symphonies and piano concertos were performed during a month of the Beethoven Festival. Under his baton, the entire *Ring Cycle* will be completed in September 2000.

One of the more lighthearted activities the Sydney Symphony Orchestra has initiated is its Toy Symphony. Groups are invited to join the Sydney Symphony Orchestra for a 30-minute rehearsal of Leopold Mozart's *Toy Symphony* in the Concert Hall. With no prior musical knowledge required, the conductor divides the Toy Orchestra into sections, gives them a rhythm and leads the group through the score. The music is carried by the string quartet of the Sydney Symphony musicians and in the end they almost sound in tune!

In 1985 Musica Viva, in conjunction with the Sydney Opera House Trust and the Festival of Perth, presented Russian violinist Igor Oistrakh and the London Philharmonia Orchestra in the Concert Hall under the direction of Klaus Tennstedt. The concert was hailed as a milestone.

The Australian Chamber Orchestra under the direction of Richard Tognetti has gone from strength to strength since its birth in 1975. It consists of a core of 17 strings, most of whom are young — the average age is less than 30. It is this that has given the company its reputation for energy and vigour in everything from eighteenth-century Gluck to modern Australian works by Peter Sculthorpe. Many notable soloists have appeared with the Orchestra over the years such as John Williams, Anthony Halstead, Yvonne Kenny, Barry Tuckwell and Lorraine Hunt, as well as conductors Sir Charles Mackerras, Frans Bròggen, Christopher Hogwood, Ton Koopman and

Marc Minkowski. In 1999, cellist Pieter Wispelwey played Shostakovich's first cello concerto in a memorable performance.

Sydney Philharmonia Choir presents its own annual concert series at the Sydney Opera House as well as acting as chorus for the Sydney Symphony Orchestra. It has been under the direction of Antony Walker since 1992. Two of its most popular pieces are Carl Orff's *Carmina Burana* and Bach's *St Matthew's Passion*.

After 17 years, the Mostly Mozart series of concerts came to an end in 1997. The series was modelled on the Mostly Mozart Concerts in New York. The idea was to create an informal atmosphere — 'Mostly Mozart, Barely Bach and Never Neckties'. It started with a few concerts in the Concert Hall but was soon extended to include free lunchtime concerts, seminars, a program of Sunday concerts and even an annual buskers' competition. In its 1996 series, the program was based on Mozart's works from 1787 to 1789 and the centenary of the birth of Dimitri Shostakovich. Maxim Shostakovich came to conduct his father's *Symphony No. 9*. He had conducted the same symphony at the Opera House in 1975 when he had to interrupt his tour to fly home on hearing of his father's death.

Over the years the Concert Hall has seen many great orchestras and ensembles perform, including Emma Kirkby and the Australian Brandenburg Orchestra Ensemble in 1996, the Nash Ensemble of London in 1997 and the purely percussion group Synergy. The world-famous The Academy of St Martin's-in-the-Field gave two concerts in the Concert Hall and played to capacity houses in 1983. The Tallis Scholars, The Choir of King's College, the London Philharmonia Orchestra, the USSR State Symphony Orchestra, the London Symphony Orchestra … the list is endless.

The youthful Australian Chamber Orchestra lying around. This orchestra has gone from strength to strength, carving a place for itself among the international musical elite. (Photo: Greg Barrett, courtesy of Australian Chamber Orchestra)

Ballet and dance

The home of The Australian Ballet is in Melbourne but each year it has a season in Sydney, usually in the Opera Theatre. The Ballet has mainly a classical repertoire, with works such as *Coppelia, Don Quixote, Swan Lake* and the twentieth century classic *Spartacus,* but it also commissions and performs new contemporary works. The Australian Ballet's first season at the Opera House began with *Sleeping Beauty,* produced by Sir Robert Helpmann with choreography by Dame Peggy van Praagh. Lucette Aldous danced the title role.

Nutcracker, choreographed by Graeme Murphy in 1992, has been a big success for the Australian Ballet. Murphy set it in the Melbourne suburbs, during a typical hot dry Christmas. The ballet revolves around the elderly ballerina Clara who, when touring Australia with the Basil Ballet Russe, finds herself trapped when the Second World War breaks out. Act II starts with the Nutcracker Overture on the radio, which sets Clara recalling her past as a dancer in pre-Revolution Russia, followed by her leaving Russia and the death of her lover. It ends with her reaching the

Above and opposite: two very successful ballets performed by the Sydney Dance Company, Salome *with Tracey Carrodus and Josef Brown and* Air and Other Invisible Forces *with Catherine Griffiths and Kip Gamblin. (Photos: Branco Gaica)*

Top right: The modern ballet, Red Earth. *Right: The classic ballet* The Merry Widow *(original production by Sir Robert Helpmann) with Marilyn Rowe. Both ballets were performed by the Australian Ballet. (Photos: Branco Gaica)*

peak of her career. Miranda Coney danced the young Clara and Margaret Scott the elderly Clara with Steven Heathcote as the lover.

One of the favourites with audiences is, of course, *Swan Lake* — it's a favourite the world over. It was *Swan Lake* that led to the first full-length ballet being performed by the Australian Ballet in the Concert Hall in 1982. Though the Concert Hall had been used on many previous occasions for contemporary dance, all ballet programs had been staged in the Opera Theatre up to then. The most popular production of *Swan Lake* came a little later in 1991 when the late Anne Woolliams returned from Europe expressly to put on her version of the famous ballet. It wasn't to everybody's liking: Woolliams had given the ballet a happy ending. By 1998, the Australian Ballet had performed the ballet 235 times.

In 1994, the Australian Ballet added the classical *Manon* to its repertoire. *Manon*, though composed in the twentieth century by Kenneth MacMillan, is about a famous Parisian courtesan in the eighteenth century. Critics praised the lavish production and fine dancing, but some felt the story line a bit old-fashioned for the 1990s.

Another classic in the Australian Ballet's repertoire is *The Merry Widow*, which was originally produced by Sir Robert Helpmann in 1975. It has always been very popular and has had many return seasons, including the 2000 season.

Not all the repertoire is classical by any means and it has grown even less so in recent years. In 1993 the ballet performed a program of some 1978 choreographed works by Jiri Kylian, including *Sinfonietta*, music by Janácek; the highly popular *Symphony D*, music by Haydn; *Nuages,* music by Debussy; and *Forgotten Land,* music by Benjamin Britten.

In 1997, Ross Stretton, a former company principal, became artistic director, taking over from Maina Gielgud. Maina Gielgud's last season as artistic director was a high point for Australian choreography, featuring a very exciting all-Australian triple bill: *The Deep End* by Meryl Tankard; Stephan Page's *Alchemy*; and Stanton Welch's *Red Earth*.

With Stretton's appointment came a fresh choreographic approach influenced by his years as assistant director of American Ballet Theatre — more contemporary choreography but still based on classical technique — as reflected in introducing a Twyla Tharp ballet, *In the Upper Room*, in his 1997 season. In 1999 Sydney audiences saw Stephan Page's 1997 production of *Rites*, a joint production of the Australian Ballet and Bangarra Dance Theatre. The ballet infused traditional European ballet with Australian indigenous culture. Unfortunately, however, it seems Stretton may be moving to the Royal Ballet in 2001 to become artistic director.

The Australian Ballet has performed over the years many contemporary ballets including: *Sand Siren* with music by Paul Gigor and Arvo Part and choreographed by Gideon Obarzanek; the vigorous and bold *In the Middle, Somewhat Elevated* by William Forsythe; and *Of Blessed Memory*, a touching tribute by resident choreographer Stanton Welch to his ballerina mother Marilyn Jones. In 1998 a little gem by Natalie Weir called *Dark Lullaby* became part of the Australian Ballet's repertoire. One critic wrote: 'Weir has created something fresh, moving and derivative of nobody but herself'.

Modern dance has always been an important element at the Opera House. In the early days the forerunner of the successful Sydney Dance Company, The Dance Company of New South Wales had their first seaon at the Opera House in November 1973. In 1976 Graeme Murphy was appointed artistic director of the Sydney Dance Company, turning it into Australia's premier modern dance company. He has choreographed no less than 40 original

Ross Stretton, artistic director of the Australian Ballet since 1997. (Photo: Jim McFarlane)

works for the Sydney Dance Company, and other works for the Australian Ballet.

The Sydney Dance Company has had many outstanding successes and has particularly attracted youthful audiences to the Opera House. *Salome* in 1998 was a resounding success; some believed it was Graeme Murphy's best work. The *Sun Herald* critic wrote: 'Graeme Murphy's *Salome* is a feast for the senses, an exotic fusion of sound, light, colour, texture and movement that results in a mesmerising interpretation of this haunting biblical tale'. Two years earlier Murphy had had a great success with his *Free Radicals*. The music for both ballets was created by Michael Askill, a percussionist who had worked with Murphy on the 1992 landmark production of *Synergy with Synergy*, a collaboration with the well-known percussion group Synergy, and again in 1999 on *Air and Other Invisible Forces*.

Apart from seasons performed by the Australian Ballet and the Sydney Dance Company, visiting ballet companies such as the Stuttgart Ballet, the Netherlands Dans Theater, Merce Cunningham, the Parsons Dance Company and many others perform at the Opera House.

Drama

The Sydney Theatre Company was born in the Opera House out of the Old Tote Theatre Company in 1978. It is the principal drama company at the Opera House and shares the Drama Theatre with the Sydney Dance Company. The Drama Theatre was originally intended as a flexible space for experimental theatre. The proscenium has the dimensions of a cinema with a very wide stage that is shallow with little space for set changes. Over the years the Drama Theatre has challenged the skills of many designers.

The Sydney Theatre Company's first season in 1979 commenced with *A Cheery Soul*, *The Lady of the Camelias* and *The Devil's Disciple*. But perhaps its most memorable early production was in 1981 with *Cyrano de Bergerac*. Written by French playwright Edmond Rostand, translated by Louis Nowra and directed by Richard Wherrett, it included an unforgettable performance by John Bell in the title role. In the same year, the musical *Chicago* was also a smash hit and starred Nancye Hayes as Roxy. It was such a success that it

Above left: Colin Friels seated as Macbeth with Eden Gaha (left) and Peter Carroll. Left: Third World Blues by David Williamson with Joel Edgerton, Jack Finsterer and Odile Le Clezio. Above: Russell Cheek in Tartuffe directed by Barry Kosky — a flamboyant production that had the Sydney theatre-going public divided. (Photos: Tracy Schramm)

John Bell as Cyrano de Bergerac in the the highly successful 1981 production at the Drama Theatre. (Photo: Brian Geach) Opposite: Jacqueline McKenzie with Luciano Martucci in Gail Edwards' production of Shaw's St Joan in the Drama Theatre, 1995. (Photo: Tracy Schramm)

transferred to Sydney's Theatre Royal for a further season.

One of the principles of the Sydney Theatre Company has always been to perform Australian plays. *What if You Died Tomorrow* by popular Australian playwright David Williamson was actually the second play performed by the Old Tote Company in its first season at the Opera House in 1973. Many of Williamson's plays have since been staged in the Drama Theatre.

Well-known novelist Thomas Keneally,

the author of *Schindler's List*, saw his play *Gossip From the Forest* performed at the Drama Theatre in 1983. A young Mel Gibson appeared in 1980 playing a Second World War soldier in *No Names, No Pack Drill. Away* by Michael Gow has been a most successful Australian play and has had repeat seasons at the Sydney Theatre Company and many performances with other companies.

Patrick White, apart from being an Australian Nobel Laureate of Literature, wrote many plays, some of which have been performed at the Opera House. His play *Season at Sarsaparilla* is an example where the designer, Brian Thomson, made full use of the wide stage, placing the three houses in which all the action takes place side-by-side across the stage as if in a street.

The classics are frequently performed, including *Macbeth* starring Colin Friels, *Comedy of Errors* with a most unforgettable Magritte-like set, the French play *Tartuffe* directed by Barry Kosky, whose production was either loved or hated, and *She Stoops to Conquer* with Leo McKern of *Rumpole* fame. In 1995 Gale Edwards directed a robust and very exciting *Saint Joan* starring the unforgettable Jacqueline McKenzie in the title role.

Alan Ayckbourn and David Hare are always favourites with audiences. In 1982 David Hare's *A Map of the World*, directed by David Hare himself and starring guest artist Roshan Seth, was an exciting and fine production.

Bell Shakespeare Company, a relatively new company founded by John Bell and Anna Volska in 1991, has, despite some financially difficult times, carved itself a niche in the theatre market by staging the classics, among which Shakespeare dominates. Often these productions give a new and vital interpretation to these well-known and frequently performed plays. When in Sydney they have, over the past few years, been performing in the Playhouse at the Opera House. One of their most exciting productions at the Playhouse has been *Coriolanus* directed by renowned guest director Steven Berkoff. The 2000 Olympic Arts Festival includes Bell Shakespeare's *Troilus and Cressida* directed by Michael Bogadanov, an acclaimed interpreter of Shakespeare.

Over the years the Playhouse has been the venue for other theatre companies, like the Ensemble Theatre, which took up residence for six months in 1983 while their own premises in Milsons Point were being renovated, and Peter and Ellen Williams Productions. Both these companies catered to a mainstream audience, with Peter and Ellen Williams concentrating in particular on popular English comedies, such as *Arsenic and Old Lace,* starring June Bronhill and Gwen Plumb, which did sell-out business.

Aboriginal performance

The Sydney Opera House is built on an Aboriginal site known as Jubgalee. It therefore seems fitting that some attention should be given to the most notable performances staged by Australia's first inhabitants.

There have not been very many indigenous programs at the Opera House. But those that have been put on range from the traditional to the contemporary, and until very recently have been almost all dance and music. It wasn't until 1997 that a full program of Aboriginal performance was seen at the Opera House. As part of the Festival of the Dreaming, the first cultural festival of the Sydney Olympics 2000, the performances aimed at presenting a dynamic view of Aboriginal life, both in its traditional and contemporary forms, and to place before audiences an honest, broad view of modern life for Aboriginals — from the dismal and tragic to the humorous and optimistic. The Festival lasted three weeks and took place in venues throughout Sydney. It began with a cleansing by smoke and an awakening of the spirits on the forecourt of the Opera House. Fifteen thousand people watched this extraordinary awakening ceremony.

In the following days, a varied program of drama as well as dance took place in the Opera House. *Black River,* the first opera to have an Aboriginal as the main character, was performed in the Concert Hall. The music was by Andrew Schultz and libretto by Julianna Schultz with Mroochy Barambah singing the role of Miriam. *Black River* takes place in a country town where a judge has arrived to investigate Aboriginal deaths in custody. While there he meets an Aboriginal mother who has lost the two most important men in her life in a single day. Another important performance given in the Concert Hall was the *Edge of the Sacred,* which was a collaboration between the Sydney Symphony Orchestra under the baton of Edo de Waart and the Aboriginal and Islander Dance Theatre. The music was by Peter Sculthorpe and included his *Kakadu, Earth Cry* and *From Uluru.*

Wimmin's Business, a collection of seven solo performances by indigenous women from Australia, Canada, the United States and New Zealand, was an exciting series of nights in the Playhouse. All very different, they each showed the strengths

The Awakening Ceremony *performed on 14 September 1996. Choreographed by Stephan Page, it enraptured an audience of 15,000 people on the Opera House forecourt. (Photo: James Pozarak)*

of storytelling in traditional society.

Fish, presented by the Bangarra Dance Theatre in the Drama Theatre, received rave reviews. Director and choreographer Stephan Page with music by David Page put on a show which was partly traditional dance and partly modern funk and was, according to Jill Sykes, just 'spellbinding'.

The Sydney Opera House is a performing arts centre where the latest in the arts is explored and performed along with the best of the traditional and the classical. Not just a spectacular building, it has become a defining focal point for the arts in Sydney. For Sydney to be without it is impossible to imagine.

'It is very possible that Australia, somewhat in spite of itself and to its own astonishment, is in the process of creating one of the great artistic wonders of the world. As the Sydney Opera House it is misnamed, but what does a name matter compared to the magnificent fact of its creation?'

George Johnston, in Robert
Goodman's book
The Australians

Running the Opera House

The Sydney Opera House Trust was set up under the *Sydney Opera House Trust Act* of 1961. It is responsible for maintenance; management and administration of the House as a performing arts and conference centre; the promotion of the cultural arts and the encouragement of new and improved forms of entertainment and methods of presentation. It has nine members, including the chairperson, and its chief executive is the general manager of the Opera House. The Trust employs 218 permanent staff and 378 casual staff.

The Trust's policy is generally to hire out the halls to other organisations who produce shows and concerts. The principal clients of the Opera House are Musica Viva Australia, the Sydney Symphony Orchestra, Opera Australia, the Australian Ballet, the Sydney Theatre Company, the Australian Chamber Orchestra, and the Bell Shakespeare Company.

The Opera House is at the hub of most festivities in Sydney: here the harbour ferries, gaily festooned for their part in the famous Australia Day Ferrython, race past it. (Photo: Geoff Ambler, courtesy of Australian Tourist Commission)

Left: The Opera House on New Year's Eve 1999 surrounded by fireworks ushering in the new millennium. (Photo: Andrew Taylor, Sydney Morning Herald)

Below left: Dressing up the Opera House: when Sydney won the Olympics, the Opera House donned the Olympic livery. (Photo: Courtesy of M.R. Hornibrook Pty Ltd) Below: The Opera House was lit up in kaleidescope colours to celebrate the arrival of the new millennium. (Photo: Nick Moir, Sydney Morning Herald)

The Trust also puts on performances that complement the activities of its major hirers. It aims to present a diverse mix of performances, and often promotes free or low-cost performances during the day, including folk and ethnic performances, children's events, etc. Also, the Trust runs educational tours of the centre for youth groups and schools, and participates in the Festival of Sydney.

The Sydney Opera House Trust has seven aims: to be a leader in cultural development; to provide first-class venues for performances of all types; to increase and diversify audiences; to create a service-oriented and dynamic workplace; to maintain and improve the architectual masterpiece, to achieve outstanding business results and to develop and promote The Sydney Opera House brand.

Maintaining the Opera House

Maintaining the Opera House is an enormous task and very expensive. Besides regularly cleaning the windows, interior and exterior light bulbs are continually replaced as are damaged roof tiles. The roof tiles are surveyed by maintenance crew who walk on the spines of the roofs along specially constructed ridge beams, also called 'ski-runs'. Safety harnesses are essential as winds coming off the harbour can be very strong. The runs are reached from a series of lofts, tunnels and manholes, and the climb to the top of the highest shell takes around an hour. When a faulty or missing tile is discovered, a member of the maintenance crew is lowered from these ridges in a safety chair to replace it. Fortunately this happens quite rarely, though 8500 tiles were recently replaced as part of a general spruce-up prior to the Sydney Olympics.

In 1988 a big upgrade program was undertaken which was to cost $113 million over 12 years. By 1995 $78 million had already spent of the allocated money. One of the continual and major problems encountered over the years has been the erosion and decay of the cement on the eastern and northern broadwalks. In 1995 it was decided to fill in the spaces in the foundations with solid concrete up to the high tide level. The deeper and steeper western side was given cathodic protection to inhibit the rusting and expansion of the reinforced steel causing the concrete to break up.

Funding the Opera House

The last Opera House Lottery was drawn in September 1986 — No. 867. Today the government pays around 25 per cent of the Opera House's running costs; this is down from around 29 per cent in earlier years. The government also contributed about $21 million in capital grants for the maintenance and upgrading of the building in 1998/1999.

The revenue comes from hiring the venues, from collecting a percentage of all ticket sales, and from the concession for souvenir shops, cafes and restaurants. Of course, the true earning power of the Opera House is inestimable. Indirectly, as a tourist attraction, it brings in millions of dollars to Australia. As well, it has hoisted Sydney onto the world stage and played a major part in the coming of age of this harbourside city.

The entrance foyer on the south side of the Opera House. (Photo: Courtesy of H.R. Hornibrook Pty Ltd)

The influence of Mayan architecture on Utzon is seen in the way the sails grow from the massive podium. (Photo: Anne Fraser)

'As an icon, it rivals the Eiffel Tower, Taj Mahal and the Pyramids, and its profile must be almost as familiar as Muhammad Ali's face or a Coca-Cola bottle. Add to this its new role as first in the lineage of spectacular 'signature' buildings designed to put places on the map . . . and Sydney is attracting almost as much attention as when Jørn Utzon won the competition half a century ago.'

Richard Weston, in The Journal of the Royal Institute of British Architects, *February 2000*

The Opera House in the New Millennium

The Sydney Opera House is the 'true millennium building', according to Richard Weston, Professor of Architecture at Cardiff University. When anyone is asked to nominate the great works of architecture of this century, he wrote 'only one twentieth century building looms large: the Sydney Opera House'. Writing in the *Journal of the Royal Institute of British Architects*, he compared it to the Eiffel Tower and the Taj Mahal in terms of its power as an icon, 'far transcending its would-be rivals in the spectacular building stakes, such as Gehry's Guggenheim'. He also paid tribute to Utzon's 'collaborative, research-based' approach to design. Although this method of working was criticised, and Utzon's great genius was shabbily treated in his last year as architect of the House, today there is a renewed relationship between the brilliant architect and the Sydney Opera House.

In 1998, the Mayor of Sydney, Frank Sartor, presented Utzon with the Keys to the City of Sydney.

In July, 1998, the Lord Mayor of Sydney, Frank Sartor, presented the Keys to the City of Sydney to Jørn Utzon. In his announcement of the honour, the Lord Mayor said: 'The Sydney Opera House has exceptional iconic value to Sydney. It is perhaps the most instantly and internationally recognised symbolic embodiment of our city ... Beyond symbolism, its design, its engineering and its location have seen the Sydney Opera House lauded as a Wonder of the Modern World'. Accepting the keys in a small ceremony on Majorca, where Utzon lives, the 80-year-old architect said that his years in Sydney working on the Sydney Opera House were the 'most wonderful' in his architectural life. But his acceptance of this award was only the beginning of a renewed relationship.

The most important development to affect the Opera House in the new millennium is Utzon's acceptance of Premier Carr's invitation to act as design consultant in any future changes to the building. In the quest to 'reunite the man and his masterpiece', Utzon will work on a 'Statement of Design Principles' which will serve as a long-term reference for the conservation and management of the building. Utzon responded to the invitation with a generous and warm letter, saying: 'This is a very important consultancy brief for me. It is a wonderful opportunity to play a further role in the life of this building, which has been an inseparable part of my life ... It is right that we should be looking forward to the future of the Sydney Opera House, and not back to the past.'

Unfortunately Utzon himself will not come to Australia but his son, Jan Utzon, will assist in a number of planned improvements. These include acoustics in the performing spaces, lighting, visitor amenities, and improved access, in particular for those who are disabled. Regretfully, Utzon has not been able to visit the Opera House, but his son and daughter have both seen it.

Approaches to the Opera House

Over the last few years there has been an enormous amount of upgrading of the approaches to the Opera House, but one change that has caused furious passions has been the construction of the apartment block dubbed 'The Toaster'. The building has caused vigorous debate, and been criticised by many who would have preferred an open space on such a sensitive site. It is a smart apartment block and an improvement on what had previously stood on the site but its drawback is that it cuts off the view of the Opera House along the main approach, managing to hide the spectacular building from anyone walking towards it from Circular Quay. However, on street level, the new restaurants and cafés have added a liveliness to the area.

The Utzon Foundation

This view of the approaches to the House was captured in 1961 by Wolfgang Sievers. (Photo: Circular Quay Towards Bennelong Point, copyright Wolfgang Sievers, 1961, reproduced with permission of Viscopy Ltd, Sydney 2000)

Designed to be an enduring tribute to Utzon, the Utzon Foundation has been one more step in the path to reconciliation with the architect. In 1998 the New South Wales Ministry for the Arts, the City of Sydney and the Sydney Opera House Trust together created a new body, the Utzon Foundation. Apart from honouring his enormous achievement in designing the Sydney Opera House, the Foundation encourages outstanding creativity in the performing arts, aims to make Sydney an international cultural centre and fosters artistic exchanges between Australia and other countries

The Foundation's aims include presenting a biennial prize for outstanding achievement for a body of work representing at least five years, awarded to an artist for a 'unique creative response to the artistic challenge', and The Sydney Opera House Awards for artists who have 'consistently excelled in their contribution to performances at the Sydney Opera House under the auspices of the major presenters'. Finally, the Foundation was created to present forums, lectures and conferences which 'explore the role of creativity in the arts and society'.

A World Heritage building?

The Sydney Opera House has not yet been nominated for inclusion on the list of World Heritage-protected buildings, but movements towards this goal have been made. In 1998, Utzon, in the TV documentary *The Edge of the Possible,* pleaded with the Federal Government to place it on the list. Because of the possibility that the New South Wales Government would thus lose control of the Opera House, the proposal was delayed. However, the Trust announced in August 1999 that Dr James Kerr had been engaged to update the conservation plan for the building, and to support efforts to gain World Heritage nomination and listing.

The innovative character of the Sydney Opera House is apparent in its design, engineering, use of technology in construction, industrialisation and standardisation of construction, and the way it used modular sections in construction. It was one of the first projects to use computers extensively, and it is one of the very few buildings in the world to become a symbol of its homeland. Architecture today is different because of Utzon; Sydney itself is different.

Today, under Utzon's guiding hand, there is further hope that the interiors may conform just a little more to his design principles. The Opera House is a performing centre for the twenty-first century, and promises to fulfil the vision it inspires spectacularly.

While explaining his design, Utzon once said: 'The sun, the light and the clouds will make it a living thing ... You never get tired, you will never be finished with it'. Visitors to Sydney may never realise the truth of this, but those who live in Sydney, especially those who see the building daily in its different moods know just how right Utzon was. Light and shadow renew the Opera House's appeal each day, highlighting its exquisite organic beauty. Magnificent in its powerful simplicity, it is indeed a timeless jewel of architecture.

CHRONOLOGY

November 1954: Premier Cahill announces that his government will build an opera house in Sydney and appoints a committee to find a suitable site.

May 1955: Committee recommends Bennelong Point for the Opera House.

August 1955: International design competition announced.

January 1956: Registration of entrants begins; judging panel chosen, and rules of criteria for inclusion set.

December 1956: Competition closes.

January 1957: Jørn Utzon selected as winner and invited to Sydney to discuss project with the State Government. Cost estimated at $7 million.

30 July 1957: Utzon first visits Sydney; presents government with initial plans.

August 1957: Opera House Executive Committee formed with 10 members and under it, the Technical Advisory Panel and the Music and Drama Advisory Panel.

March 1958: Utzon presents *Red Book* to government plans and notes.

August 1958: Demolition of the Fort Macquarie tram depot begins.

November 1958: Civil & Civic P/L wins tender for Stage 1: foundations and podium.

2 March 1959: Foundations are started for Stage I. Utzon and Cahill lay foundation stone.

October 1959: Premier Cahill dies in office.

March 1960: *Sydney Opera House Act* passed by Parliament, approving expenditure of $9.6 million, the new cost estimate.

January 1962: Utzon presents government with *Yellow Book*.

March 1963: Utzon and family move to Sydney.

April 1963: Stage I is finalised; Stage II, construction of the shells, begins.

August 1963: Additional expenditure up to $25 million is approved in Parliament.

November 1963: First rib section mounted.

June 1964: Cost estimates rise to $35 million.

May 1965: Coalition of Liberal-Country Party wins government in New South Wales after campaigning on platform alleging Labor mismanagement of Opera House funding. Davis Hughes (Country Party) made Minister for Public Works.

28 February 1966: Jørn Utzon resigns; roofs largely completed.

March 1966: Demonstrations over Utzon leaving.

7-10 March 1966: Meetings between Utzon and Hughes take place; Hughes proposes that Utzon return in charge of design only.

17 March 1966: Utzon declines the offer, makes counter-proposals which are refused by the government.

19 April 1966: State Government appoints Todd, Hall and Littlemore under government architect Ted Farmer to complete construction

28 April 1966: Utzon and family leave Australia.

June 1966: Utzon received Gold Honour Medal of West German Architects' Association for the Sydney Opera House design.

January 1967: Panel presents 'Review of Program' to State Government.

March 1967: New design is approved, and Stage III, the internal fittings and approaches, is started. M.R. Hornibrook Pty Ltd contracted to do paving and cladding: cost $56.5 million.

March 1968: In an interview with the *Australian* newspaper, Utzon offers to return to Sydney under mutually acceptable terms. The offer is ignored.

20 October 1973: Official opening by Her Majesty Queen Elizabeth II. Final cost comes to $102 million.

1973: Utzon awarded Gold Medal of the Royal Australian Institute of Architects.

1978: Utzon awarded Gold Medal of the Royal Institute of British Architects.

1982: Utzon receives Alvar Aalto Medal from Finland.

January 1988: New forecourt and lower concourse completed under auspices of NSW Department of Public Works in association with Hall Bowe and Webber: cost $62 million.

August 1990: Twelve-storey car park with 1100 spaces contracted out to Enacon Parking P/L: cost $40 million.

March 1993: Car park opened.

March 1993: Plaque with spherical solution for roof design is unveiled, honouring Utzon.

19 June 1998. Utzon pleads with the Federal Government to put the Sydney Opera House on World Heritage Listing.

July 1998: Jørn Utzon presented with Keys to the City of Sydney by Sydney's Lord Mayor, Frank Sartor, in Majorca.

October 1998: Twenty-fifth anniversary of Sydney Opera House: Utzon Foundation established to honour Utzon and to award prizes in the arts.

March 1999: The Studio, the new venue for contemporary performing arts, opens, along with an adjoining western foyer connecting the Drama Theatre and Playhouse.

August 1999: Utzon accepts a brief to prepare a Statement of Design Principles to guide any further work on the building, as part of a new Strategic Plan for the Sydney Opera House to be written by Richard Johnson of Denton Corker Marshall.

31 December 1999: Millennium celebrations at the Opera House.

BIBLIOGRAPHY

Adams, Brian, *Portrait of an Artist: A Biography of William Dobell*, Hutchinson Group (Australia) Pty Ltd, Richmond, Victoria, Australia 1983.

Annual Report, Sydney Opera House Trust, 1999.

Arup, Ove and Jack Zunz, *Sydney Opera House: A paper on its design and construction,* Sydney Opera House Trust; Sydney 1988.

Baume, Michael, *The Sydney Opera House Affair*,Thomas Nelson (Australia) Ltd, Sydney, 1967.

Bonyge, Richard, *Joan Sutherland and Richard Bonynge with the Australian Opera*, Craftsman Press, Sydney, 1990.

Brisbane, K. (ed.), *Entertaining Australia:An Illustrated History*,Currency Press, Sydney, 1991.

Cargher, J., *Opera and Ballet in Australia*, Cassell Australia, Sydney, 1977.

Cargher, J., *Bravo! Two Hundred Years of Opera in Australia*, Macmillan Australia, Sydney, 1988.

Curtis, Robert Emerson, *A Vision Takes Form: a graphic record of the building of the Sydney Opera House during Stage One and Two,* A.H. & A.W. Reed, Sydney, 1967.

De Vries, Susanna, *Historic Sydney: The Founding of Australia,* 3rd edition. Pandanus Press, Brisbane,1999

Drew, Philip, *Sydney Opera House: Jorn Utzon*, Architecture in Detail series, Phaidon Press Ltd, London, 1995.

Drew, Philip, *The Masterpiece,* Hardie Grant Books, South Yarra, 1999.

Elias Duek-Cohen, *Utzon and the Sydney Opera House: a statement in the public interest,* Sydney, 1967.

Formby, D., *Australian Ballet and Modern Dance,*Lansdowne Press, Sydney, 1981.

Fromonot, Francoise, *Jorn Utzon: The Sydney Opera House*, Gingko Press Inc, Corte Madera, California, 1998.

Goodman, Robert, text by George Johnston, *The Australians*, Rigby, Adelaide, 1966.

Hall, H. & A. Cripps, *Romance of the Sydney Stage*, Currency Press with National Library of Australia, 1996.

Hubble, Ava (ed.), *Sydney Opera House: Grand Organ, Specification and Background Notes,* Publicity Department of the Sydney Opera House, Sydney, 1980.

Hubble, Ava, *More than Just an Opera House*, Publicity Department of the Sydney Opera House, Sydney.

Hubble, Ava, *Sydney Opera House: More than Meets the Eye*, Lansdowne Press 1983.

Kiri Te Kanawa with Conrad Wilson, *Opera for Lovers,* Hodder & Stoughton, Sydney 1996

Marr, David (ed.), *Patrick White: Letters*, Random House Australia, 1984.

Messent, David, *Opera House Act On,*David Messent Photography, Sydney 1997.

Sim, James, *Sydney Opera House*, View Productions, Sydney 1983.

Smith, Michael Pomeroy, *Sydney Opera House,* William Collins Pty Ltd, Sydney, 1984.

Smith, Vincent, *The Sydney Opera House,* Paul Hamlyn, Sydney, 1974.

Sykes, Jill, *Sydney Opera House: from the outside in,* Playbill, Pymble, 1993.

The Hornibrook Group, *Building the Sydney Opera House*, The Hornibrook Group, a division of Wood Hall Ltd, Sydney, 1973.

Turnbull Hughes, Lucy, *Sydney: Biography of a City*, Random House Australia, Sydney, 1999.

Watkin, David, *A History of Western Architecture*, 2nd Edition, Laurence King, London 1996.

Yeomans, John, *The Other Taj Mahal*, Longmans, Green and Co Ltd, London, 1968.

Sources on the Net

Australia's Cultural Network: www.acn.net.au/articles/1998/10/soh.htm

Official The Australian Ballet Web Site: www.austballet.telstra.com.au

Official Opera Australia Web Site: www.opera-australia.org.au

Official Sydney Opera House Web Site: www.soh.nsw.gov.au

Official Sydney Symphony Orchestra Web Site: www.symphony.org.au

INDEX